A Market Mans Tale

By Daniel Howard Mulcahy

Table of Contents

Prologue
4

Chapter 1 Aunt Kitty to the rescue
5

Chapter 2 Our Hanna's arrival
9

Chapter 3 I Begin School
14

Chapter 4 The Forging of friendships
17

Chapter 5 Some of the shops and neighbour's of the Market26

Chapter 6 Dundrum School Trip
30

Chapter 7 Defying the Ivy Gang and a cycle to Dundalk   37

Chapter 8 Coming of age and the pubs are a beckoning   45

Chapter 9 Bennie Beattie and Maggie Elder
54

Chapter 10 Working in the bakery
59

Chapter 11 Honeymoon from Hell
66

Chapter 12 The railroad squad
76

Chapter 13 Geordie Stow is as fly as they go
82

Chapter 14 From freedom to slavery (marriage)
85

Chapter 15 Our family begins
92

Chapter 16 Some old mates drinkers and punters the lot   96

Chapter 17 The troubles break out
99

Chapter 18 The partition of Ireland
105

Chapter 19 The creation and maintenance of an artificial

State
110

Chappter 21 Dan Mulcahy versus Usain Bolt 120

Chapter 22 More additions to the clan and life resumes a   125   normal

Chapter 23 The exploits of Captain Crook 127

Chapter 24 Five rockets caught up in rocket attack at the   133

Rock
Chapter 25 The old Market is replaced by the new 136

Chapter 26 Two very different women 138

Chapter 27 A family reunion 141

Chapter 28 A great community spirit 143

Chapter 29 To hell and back 147

Prologue

The Market's area of Belfast situated in the south side of the city, just a short stroll from the city Centre is were I was reared. Although if you were fortunate enough to know it back in the day you will be only too aware that the Market's of today would be unrecognizable if you were to stroll through it presently. Gone are the cattle yards, the old streets with their cobble stones and pavements, the old shops and pubs and the rows of two up two down terraced houses with their outside toilets and where an open fire was our only source of heat and which in many a case would house a family of ten or more. Does it sound like hard times? Sure they were hard times but it wasn't all doom and gloom and the people of the Market's were and still are the salt of the earth. I possess a great pride of the fact that I was reared in the Market's and unfortunately many of the old residents and characters of the area have passed away or moved on. Now I'm sure there are a lot of young folk out there in all walks of life who have heard many a tale relayed to them by their elders who were brought up in the area but can only form a picture in their minds of how it really was. They may have pride in the fact that they are the new generation of Market people or in the fact that their parents originated from the Market's whilst they themselves were not born and reared in the area and well you should have pride. I certainly hope you can join me on my journey through the old Market's and learn of some of the places and streets that have long since gone but especially of some of the people and characters who really make an area what it is (the people of that area). As for any of you oldies who travel on this journey it will only rekindle old memories but I hope they are pleasant ones as you join me in A Market's Mans Tale.

Chapter 1

Aunt Kitty to the rescue

It was in the year 1939 when the sky was full of lead, Hitler was heading to Poland and Paddy to Hollyhead and wee Danny Boy Mulcahy was heading down to the Markets area of Belfast. I was born on the thirteenth of November in the year of our Lord 1938 in a small red bricked terraced house in Iveagh Parade off the Falls Road near Broadway. Our family household consisted of myself, my father Henry, mother Mary and my three female siblings Marie, Bernadette and Eileen. My father Henry worked as a linesman for the General Post Office installing telephones whilst also serving as a part time soldier in the Territorial Army before eventually enlisting with the Royal Ulster Rifles as a full time soldier at the outbreak of the Second World War. Soon after enlisting he was shipped out to France where unfortunately he was killed in action and was buried in French soil as was his own father before him Daniel Mulcahy who was also killed in action during the First World War. My paternal grandfather Daniel Mulcahy hailed from the small town of Gurnard in the County of Waterford in the southeast corner of Ireland before travelling north to Belfast around the 1880s. He was reared by a protestant family by the name of Howard whom he respected greatly and it was always his wish that one of his grandchildren carry the name of Howard hence my being named Daniel Howard Mulcahy. The Mulcahy name was quite common in the Counties of Waterford, Limerick, Cork and South Tipparery in the seventeenth century as is evident by the numerous entries of the name in the census of 1659. Two characters of not who bore the Mulcahy, name, were Denis Dowling Mulcahy 1833-1900 a medical doctor and leading member of the Irish Republican Brotherhood from Redmondstown County Tipperary and Jeremiah Hodges Mulcahy an artist teacher and influential active participant in the Fenian Uprising of 1867. Upon reflection and with hindsight I firmly believe that those bloody and wasteful world wars robbed both me and my father before me of our childhoods and unfortunately for my poor father they deprived him of both his childhood and adulthood.

Soon after my father was killed our family moved to Granville Street in the Lower Falls/ Grosvoner Road area to a similar two bedroom terraced house which lay in close proximity to my Granny Mulcahy's house at 1 Milford Street where she resided with her new husband who she married a number of years after my grandfather's passing. Granny Mulcahy or Granny Masie as she was known to us had re-married to a man called Frank Grimley and a true gentleman is the best way I could describe Frank. My Granny Masey would send Frank round to our house each and every day to check on us and upon entering Frank would always address my mother saying

"Did the wee man get his beanies today?"

My diet was so poor that as a result I had developed Rickets through mal- nourishment especially calcium and vitamin D. My condition deteriorated rapidly to such an extent that after the doctor was sent for the priest soon followed and that could only mean one thing, I was on my way out and my mother remarked that only a miracle could save me at that point.

The miracle was soon to happen as there was a loud knock on our front door and when it was opened there she stood my Aunt Kitty who had come all the way up from her home in the Markets. After a brief conversation over a fresh pot of tea Aunt Kitty stated to my mother that she would bring me down to the Markets and see if she could nurse me back to health and with that she bundled me up in her arms and carted me off to her home at number nine Staunton Street. There she bathed me in rock salt which was used to cure cow and sheep hides and fed me cod liver oil, malt extract and soft eggs that were beat up in a cup with country butter. I can remember my Aunt Kitty on numerous occasions commenting that when I came down to Staunton Street that my legs looked like two straws hanging from a hay loft. Aunt Kitty was a wee stout woman with a heart of corn and lived with her husband Thomas Moore who was employed as a carter and they had no children of their own. I will freely admit that Aunt Kitty was true to her word as I was slowly nursed back to health.

Our house in number nine Staunton Street like the majority of the households in the Markets at the time possessed an outside toilet which as you can imagine was not the most comfortable during the long cold winter months. Like the majority of the small terraced houses in the Markets area at that time the only source of heating was a large open fire which was situated in the living room or as it would have been called at the time the sitting room. The front window of our house consisted of numerous smaller panes of glass each in their own little wooden frame which looked out over Staunton Street and facing Keegan Street and our house was known as the house with the wee windows. In the scullery or kitchen as it would be known today, a window looked out onto Campbell's Place and there in the corner of the scullery stood a large brown sink and that's where all the washing was done. When I was older I used to stick my kite/face under the water tap for the purpose of waking myself up in the morning and I can assure you the freezing cold water that came out did just that. There was no such a thing as central heating in them days and the only way to obtain warm water was to boil it. Even to this day I don't feel fully awake until I complete the procedure of sticking my kite under the cold tap each morning. Unlike now days where we are spoiled for choice, our only lighting source was the gas mantles placed throughout the house and we also possessed a gas poker for lighting the fire until electricity was finally installed in the late forties.

The clothes were washed in a large tin bath with the aide of a wash board made up of a corrugated type glass in which you scrubbed the clothes using a large bar of life boy soap quoting the old terminology from the TV advertisement concerning an unruly youth

"Why don't you get a life boy."

As stated this bath and wash board served as the washing machine could you imagine the young women now days taking on such a task? Upon completing a wash Aunt Kitty would empty the bath of the soapy water and refill it with fresh water for the purpose of rinsing the freshly washed clothes. She would then run them through this large mangle which consisted of two large rollers that squeezed the water from the clothes that would emerge like sheets of card board. There were no such luxuries, such as tumble dryers or washer dryers for Aunt Kitty. After the clothes had dried came the ironing and that was also an ordeal in them days. You had to place a couple of iron blocks into the fire until they were red hot and lift them out using a pair of tongs and slide them into the compartment at the base of the iron. You would smooth your clothes and when the irons cooled down you repeated the procedure of reheating them in the fire or you could place them on the gas ring of the cooker to re-heat them. Aunt Kitty's day was taken up with washing, ironing, cooking and cleaning and when they say a woman's work is never done in Aunt Kitty's day it applied big time. Now days they talk about them being the good old times well that being the case I wouldn't like to see the bad old times.

What amazed me back then was how the women of that era were able to put three meals a day on the table and clothe their children with so little income coming in as their men folk were mostly unemployed through no fault of their own. The reason for the high unemployment rate in the impoverished Nationalist/Catholic working class enclaves of Belfast at the time was due to the discriminatory practices of the old Stormont Apartheid Government of the time. To quote Sir Basil Brook when asked his opinion of Catholics at the time he stated that he would not have one about the place nor in his employ. This led to widespread discrimination against Catholics in the work place especially in the large Protestant dominated shipbuilding and engineering industries that were flourishing in the city of Belfast at the time. In the 1920s thousands of Catholic workers were forced to flee their workplaces in the shipyard and other engineering factories in many cases suffering personal physical assaults with at least one fatality being recorded. A number of Protestant workers who tried to stand by their Catholic workmates were also expelled and were labelled socialists and communists and were never re-instated.

Chapter 2

Our Hanna's arrival

Our Hannah my mother's sister came down to the Market's to live with Aunt Kitty when her own mother died at a young age, Hannah was just four years of age at the time. Aunt Kathleen my mothers sister had taken on the task of caring for her younger siblings and as you can imagine back in the day that would have been no easy job but her resilience and toughness seen her through and I hope she's in heaven if there is such a place. Our Hannah's father Billy Robinson who was also my maternal grandfather would later re-marry to a lady by the name of Maggie Hughes and they would have a son also named Billy whom I have met down through the years and now resides in Wales. In later years when Kathleen and her siblings had grown into adulthood Kathleen got married to a man named Joe Hinds and moved to a house in Varner Street right next door to my Granny Hillman which run off Lesson Street in the Lower Falls district. Kathleen's younger sister who had also married lived just a couple of doors away. Aunt Kitty now had two orphans to look after our Hannah and myself.

Aunt Kitty would purchase her meat from Shannon's butchers shop in Cromac Street were they sold nothing but grade A meat. If only the same could be said of the meat we are eating now days. Unlike now days, where the cattle are beefed up on steroid drugs and the use of chemical pesticides are more common place, the meat had a different texture in those days and the same could also be said of the poultry and pork. When you cooked the bacon back then the odour would waft all over the street. I used to watch Aunt Kitty clean out the chickens as you had to do in those days by putting her hand inside the chicken and pulling out it's innards before pour in boiling water to sterilize the inside of the chicken. Then there was the fish and Aunt Kitty would bone and gut them herself unlike now days were they are all gutted and boned for us. If I was to gut and sterilize a chicken in front of my wife Patsy she would have run a mile due to the fact that she has never eaten chicken in her life. Ah! Poor wee Patsy she doesn't know what she is missing.

Aunt Kitty most certainly put in a lot of time and effort into putting food on the table which was no easy task as her husband was retired and she now had two orphans to feed and clothe and neither my own mother nor Hannah's father would provide her with any financial assistance but she managed somehow. I can still remember some of the dishes that Aunt Kitty would put up for us as though it were yesterday. There was what Aunt Kitty called her beef tea that consisted of boiled beef and carrots, cows tongue which was skinned and pressed then boiled and was absolutely lovely with mustard. Champ made with scallions, milk, butter and spuds washed down with a glass of butter milk. Fresh liver, not that frozen crap from New-Zealand fried with onions. Oxtail soup made with real oxtail. Chicken soup made with whole chicken boiled in the large soup pot and potted herrings. It was all fresh food back then, unlike, the frozen food of the modern era, where in some instances even the bread is frozen. The tomatoes these days I call rhino tomatoes because you need a chain saw to cut through the skin. There is nothing could beat the Jersey toms or home grown tomatoes back then as they would have melted in your mouth. People talk about free range eggs, which I personally think is a big scam as the cost difference is extortionate. How does an unborn chicken in an egg know whether its mother is walking around a farm or sitting in a cage like a battery hen.

As I have previously stated, my mother would not send any money for my keep, so one fine day Aunt Kitty decided to bundle me up and bring me back up to my mother. She took our Hanna by the hand; she was six years old at the time and marched us up to

Granville Street. She knocked on the door and my mother came to the door.

"Here you keep him." Aunt Kitty shouted angrily and turned on her heels and walked out.

As she was half way down the street I began to squeal the place down. Charlie Treble my future step father tried to pacify me with a couple of spoons but this was to no avail. Aunt Kitty heard me all the way down the street, hurried back and lifted me in her arms and took me back to God's country 'The Markets.' As I was growing up my Aunt Kitty fed me cod liver oil, soft boiled eggs beat up in a cup with lots of country butter and malt sprinkled with rock salt. That coupled with her loving care slowly helped me gain my strength.

At the age of three I remember sitting on my Aunt Kitty's knee. My mother was planning to move to Liverpool with my stepfather Charlie Treble. My two sisters Marie and Bernie were playing outside my Granny Masie Mulcathy's house and my mother was speaking to my Granny about the children's welfare. My mother was asking my Granny to keep the kids with her and her husband Frank Grimley. Frank and my Granny didn't want their grandchildren to move away to Liverpool so they both agreed. Alice Mooney, my mother's cousin was outside with my two sisters when my mother walked out to them. She knelt down, hugged them close, kissed them and handed them a thruppenny bit each. With that she stood up and walked off with Alice Mooney. Our Bernie was crying after her, but without looking back she walked on until she was out of sight. Both my sisters have now passed from cancer. Down through the years Marie seemed to have got over the ordeal but our Bernie never got over it, she had to receive counselling for years after. Granny Mulcahy had already reared her family so to have to start and bring up two grandchildren was no easy task at her age.

In my younger days Aunt Kitty would get the large oval tin bath out, the same bath that she would use to wash the clothes in. She would put it by the large open fire to keep me warm and fill it up with lots of hot water from the tin buckets she was warming on the gas stove. I was five years old at the time and the war was raging on with German planes dropping bombs all over Belfast. It was decided to evacuate most of the children out of the Markets for their own safety. So we were put on lorries with Aunt Kitty putting me and our Hanna together and wrapped us up like fish suppers with coats and blankets. She lifted us on to the back of the lorry and made sure we were safely secured. It was night time, the weather was cold and we drove off into the country to safety; if memory serves me right I think it was somewhere near Ballymena, which then seemed a million miles away from war torn Belfast. Our Hanna told me later that we only stayed one night before returning home the following morning but at least we were safe from Hitler's bombers and had went on an adventure to Ballymena.

Sometimes we would hide in the coal hole which was a tiny space located under the stairs. It had a small door which was accessed from the living room and I often wondered how in the name of God a coal man could empty a bag of coal into such a small opening;

he must have been a dwarf. Like the majority of Markets households we kept our coal in the yard. Did you ever hear the old saying "It was like trying to wrestle a bear up a coal hole." This is where it came from.

Aunt Kitty worked in Makie's engineering factory on the Springfield Road during the war years of the early forties. She made shell casings for the war effort. I was around five at the time and Aunt Kitty would get her sister Maggie Dean who lived in Mc Donnell Street off the Grosvenor Road to look after me while she went to work. When the Second World War ended, she got a job in Telephone House in May Street as a cleaner. She got this job through my father who was killed in the war. She would start early in the morning at around 6.00am until 9.00am then she would return again later that evening and work from 6.00pm until 8.00pm. This meant she was able to sort the tea out for the family before finishing her shift. Aunt Kitty would always get me and our Hanna's school clothes ready the night before. Our Hanna was around thirteen at the time and would help out with the cleaning and ironing, this was a fairly typical role played by young girls at this time. Aunt Kitty would wake her up at 5.00am a couple of mornings each week and she would queue at McWatters bakery in Cromac Street with her woollen shawl wrapped around her to keep her warm. I could picture her standing in the queue like little orphan Annie waiting her turn to get the cheap bread. She had this pillow case that she would place the bread in and sling it over her shoulder. It never mattered what the weather was like our Hanna was there. On Saturdays when she was off school Aunt Kitty would send our Hanna up to Maggie Deans in Mc Donnell Street with some of the bread that she had purchased from McWatters.

Aunt Kitty would tell me and Hanna that when she attended school in her younger days on the Falls Road that some children would go to work in the mills at six in the morning until noon then attend school until four in the afternoon. They would work in their bare feet for a pittance; child slave labour I would call it. This was all done with the blessing of the Catholic Church and the rich mill owners. Back handers wouldn't have been out of place here I bet. Aunt Kitty would often take our Hanna and I visiting around the Falls Road during the early forties when the war was in full flight. Aunt Kitty loved to talk and tell stories of days gone by and I can recall Hanna and I lying beside her yawning and eventually falling asleep on many occasions but that's how history carries forward.

One night the three of us were walking down the Grosvenor Road, the streets were in darkness as there was a curfew in place. A big peeler stepped out of the shadows with his rain cape and a large torch in his hand.

He said to Aunt Kitty

"In the name of God missus then two children [referring to us] should be in their beds at this time of night."

It was twelve o'clock at night

"Do you realize there is a curfew on" he said.

"I'm standing here hoping not to get my head blew off waiting for my shift to finish and get home safe and sound. Go now" he said.

"And safe passage home." At that he disappeared back into the shadows, Aunt Kitty would repeat this story over and over throughout the years.

Sunday in our house was special as Aunt Kitty put so much effort and work into preparing the Sunday dinner. I was sent up with a jug to Larry Ford's cattle yard at the top of Eliza Street to fetch buttermilk. As soon as you entered the yard you could smell the cows manure, Larry also kept pigs, chickens and sheep, everything you would find on a farmyard. Mrs Ford would come out of the side entrance of their house which stood in Eliza Street. She was a real country type looking woman with a long apron. She would take my jug and approach this large wooden vat which stood on two pivots which were either side to allow the vat to tumble and churn the milk into butter. Mrs Ford would tilt the vat down to enable her to use a ladle to fill my jug, as the butter would be floating on the top. This butter milk was the real mc coy not like the watered stuff you get today. I know most people today won't drink the stuff saying that it's full of fat but there's not an ounce of fat in it. Back down to Aunt Kitties with the butter milk I went and sat down at the table which was placed in the living room beside the big open fire. Bowls of chicken soup in front of Aunt Kitties husband Thomas, our Hannah and me. Your dinner would follow and you washed it down with a large glass of butter milk. Your dinner consisted of chicken, vegetables and loads of potatoes; we called them pesetas, it sounded like the old Spanish currency. Aunt Kitty wouldn't let you leave the table until you had finished your dinner.

"Get that ate up or you will not grow up to be strong and healthy" she would say.

Even today whatever is set down in front of me to eat I will finish the lot although I have now moved to smaller plates.

I was about four or five years old when I walked into a classroom for the first time. It had rows of small desks, wooden floors and the walls were covered with paintings and drawings from past pupils. This was generally called the babies class by the parents and this is where your education began. Miss Wright was our teacher and I remember she would give us a lump of plastic moulding and we made wee men and whatever else we could think of apart from rolling it into balls and hitting some body up the back of the head. As the years rolled on I moved up the classes and was taught by Miss Sloan, Mr Smith, Mr Collins and Mr Donnelly who was the head teacher. Mr Smith would take our class for reading and singing. He was tall with grey hair, of thin build, wore glasses and was always well dressed with collar and tie, grey tweed coat and dark slacks. He would read all the old classics Kidnapped, Treasure Island etc. He would have a cup of tea in one hand, the book in the other and a packet of ginger biscuits. Then he would take us for singing class. We would start off with My Grandfathers Clock, which I hated, Jesus who wrote this crap. Mr Donnelly the head master would take us for maths which was not my scene. After the lesson he would collect for the children of the third world; black and white. I recall one particular occasion when it was for the white babies when Mr Donnelly came to big Finn Mulligan who was sitting at the back of the class.

"White baby money Finn" he said.

"I have no money Sir" said Finn as he looked up at the teacher. "My mummy says there's enough white babies in our house,"

"Oh is that right" said Mr Donnelly, as he went to fetch his cane.

Finn was given a few slaps on both hands but it did not fizz on the big lad.

PLACE PHOTO HERE

Picture 1 is my class photograph

On the front row from left to right we have Brendan Murdock, Tommy McCormack, Paul Collins, Gusty Forgone and the one and only Daniel Mulcahy. Brian McCusker, Billy Campbell, Francey McNally, Tommy Conlon, Jimmy Delaney, Harry Hanna, Doc Kane and Seany Craig. Seany later died tragically in a fight in Lagan Lane of Cromac Square. He died of a knife wound when he was eighteen years old. Then there is Junior Morrison, Jim McCabe and Christy Doherty who in later years was murdered by sectarian bigots as he stood in Sean Graham's bookies on the Ormeau Road. Five people died including a sixteen year old boy who was the son of Kathleen Nolan a lovely wee girl who lived three doors up from our house. Kathleen never got over his death and died a few years later. Christy and I lived in the same street and sat together in the same class in school. Christy never had a sectarian thought in his head. Then we have Mr Smith our teacher, Tommy McDonnall and Jimmy Moss who was a real character. Following them we have Jinny Kennedy, Tommy Smith Jerry Daley, Gerry Walsh, M Holden, J Scott, Toby Smith, Tommy Daley, Packy McAllister, Toc Hanna and Eugene Butler. Roger McDonald was also in my class but he wasn't in the school photo. His son Henry went on to become a top journalist with a southern newspaper; he didn't take it after Roger who couldn't spell [only joking Roger.]

My pet hates in school were Maths English and religion. The latter was especially a subject I never really cared for. I believe Religion should not be taught as a compulsory subject in schools but left as an option when the child reaches the age of reason; about seventy years old would you say? We were taught Irish language but not Irish history. As a youngster I could never understand why the old education board, which was run by the old Stormont Government would not supply any real factual history books on Irish historical figures such as Wolfe Tone or Michael Collins to catholic schools. I understand now.

Aunt Kitty would take me round to Sunday mass in St Malachy's Chapel in Alfred Street. When I was about seven years old I was kneeling and saying my prayers when she pointed up to the pews above the Alter and told me that the angels lived up there and they were looking down on us. I could see things moving around and can remember telling everyone about the angels. I later discovered it was the pigeons from St Coleman's primary school which was just around the corner in Eliza Street beside Johnny McKeown's blacksmith shop. One morning at Aunt Kitty's house I was getting up for school and I could hardly move my legs. The joints in my knees felt like the bones were rubbing together so when I got dressed our Hanna took me to the doctors. I was referred to the Royal Hospital to get checked out for arthritis; I was twelve years old and thought only old lads in their nineties got this sort of thing but it runs in my mother's side of the family. The doctors put pads on my knees which were wired up to an electric machine, with my bare feet placed in a tub of water. I was given a few jolts of twelve volts to my knees and I received this treatment on ten occasions which eventually cleared it up. From that day until now and I am now seventy three years old; I have not felt as much as twinge on my knees. I don't know whether or not they still use this treatment but it certainly worked for me.

Hannah attended the nuns convent school in Joy Street and it wouldn't be until years later that she informed us that she hadn't been treated very well by the staff because she was an orphan and God forbid if you were unfortunate enough to be born out of wedlock your fate would be even worse. The words of Jesus come to mind when he Our Lord said

"Suffer little children come on to me."

What a pity them words were not put into practice, after all what fault was it of these innocent children what their family situation was.

Chapter 4

The forging of friendships

The Lundy's lived in Keegan Street facing our house. Marie Lundy was a lovely girl and was great friends with our Hanna. They went to the same school which was a nun's convent. Her sister Eileen Lundy was also a lovely young girl and they had two brothers Eamon and Sandy. I used to go out with a lovely wee girl from the Short Strand called Rosy Lundy but she was no relation. She went on to marry someone else from the Short Strand. At the top of our street stood Barney Morrison's yard where I learned to kill and pluck chickens. One day I was standing in Keegan Street with my mate, we were around ten years old at the time. He had a mongrel dog called Dawn who got tangled up with this bitch and both dogs got locked together. People in them days would whack the dogs with floor brushes and throw buckets of cold water over them which wouldn't achieve its objective. In other words it wasn't having any effect and the poor auld mutts must have wondered what was happening to them. My mate panicked and ran into the house and came out with this razor blade. I must point out the innocence of children in those days as my mate thought it was dogs dirt that was keeping them stuck together. He went over to the dogs and started to hack the two dogs apart with the razor blade. There was blood everywhere as you can imagine and the two dogs separated immediately much to the relief of all those present. It was no relief for poor old Dawn the dog who was never the same after that ordeal and every time he seen a bitch he done a runner once bitten twice shy and all that. He died the following year a broken dog. I wonder why?

Christmas time in the Markets was something you looked forward to. The comics you read would give you a good indication that Christmas was approaching. The Beano and the Dandy would both have snowflakes drew on the front covers and a Christmas pudding with holly sticking out the top of it on the front page. In the Dandy you had Desperate Dan sitting at his table with his knife and fork waiting for his dinner and his wee Auntie Annie would come in with this giant cow pie with the horns and tail hanging over the side. How she carried that large pie with her wee spindly legs is beyond me. Desperate Dan had a wee cowboy hat and a gun strapped around his large waist. He would shave the stubble on his chin with a blow lamp. Is it any wonder the kids back then were crazy! Now getting back to cow pies, I knew a man from the Short Strand big Geordie Heaney, a docker who stood six foot five and was powerfully built and had a reputation for eating large quantities of food. He could have eaten two of these pies at one sitting no bother followed by four fish suppers out of Maggie Martin's fish and chip shop in Cromac Street. Other characters in the Dandy were Corky the Cat and Key Hole Kate and who could forget Denis the Menace, lord Snooty, Pansy Potter and many more and you also had the Hot Spur. There were no televisions, consoles, I phones or lap tops in those days. If kids were unruly in my day their parents would blame the comics.

"That's them comics they are reading" they would say. "I'm sure it has their heads away.

Young John McMullen lived a few doors up from our house. He lived with his mother wee Maggie and his sisters Marie and Rita, two lovely girls. His brothers, big Tom the Bear we called him, as he would get you in a bear hug and squeeze the life out of you and his brother Bobby. When John and I were around eight years old he called to my house with two holsters and two white guns that his uncle Jimmy McCarthy, Pat and Maura's father brought back from overseas as he was in the merchant navy. John pulled the guns out and said

"Stick them up."

I grabbed the barrels and they broke off, it seemed they were made of chalk. Poor John cried his eyes out. I tried to stick them together with tin milk as we had no superglue then, but it didn't work. Toys were scarce then so children had to be inventive. You would sometimes get two empty tins and put a string through the bottom of each tin. The string would be about fifteen to twenty feet long and you would put your ear to the tin and your mate would do like wise. When you could not hear your mate you would put the tin down and shout

"What did you say?"

Then he would shout

"Can you hear me now?"

It kind of defeated the purpose, but don't laugh because these tins were the equivalent of the modern I phones back in the fifties. Comics were your sole indoor entertainment, once you read them, you were off outside to play hand ball, skipping, football or conkers. To make a conker you inserted a heated nail through the centre of a chestnut and then you threaded a piece of string in through the hole and tied a knot. Then someone would challenge you to see whose conker could withstand the impact of the other as you held it up by the string and he would try to smash yours. If he missed then it was your turn. Some would keep their chestnuts in the drawer for a whole year in order to season them, which was a hard thing to accomplish I must say. This would make them as hard as stones and then you had a greater chance of smashing everyone else's conkers. It didn't matter what you did as long as you were active. I believe the children now days, including my own grandchildren are not exercising enough. They don't seem to realize that this will affect their joints in later years but when you tell kids now days they won't listen to you, it falls on deaf ears.

In my day your parent's word was their bond and if you were asked to do a chore or run an errand you did not hesitate. In the summer time we had six weeks of school, which meant swimming and fishing up on the Cavehill. Our makeshift rods consisted of a bamboo rod with the fishing net at the end. We would bring jam jars with us, into which we put the small spricks that we caught and when we returned home we would put bits of bread into the jars to feed the fish. The following morning I would go out to the yard to see how the fish were doing and I would find them floating on top of the jam jar dead as a door nail. In my naivety I thought it might have been something in the bread, not realizing I had stuffed too much bread in the jar and the fish couldn't breathe.

We also spent a lot of our summer holidays swimming. Spike McCormack, Chuck Conlon, Chuck's brother David who we nicknamed Dee Dee and I would head for the swimmers. I was about ten years old when I learned how to swim at the swimmers which were situated in Ormeau Avenue facing the Gas Works. There were steps at the shallow end of the pool which descended into three feet of water and this is where I would practice. Chuck and his brother Dee Dee could hardly swim but Spike on the other hand was something else. He could give you a full length full head start and pass you half way into the second lap. He used the front crawl style to great effect, tall and well-built he could fly through the water like a shark. When I look back I would say Spike was championship material, he was a natural. They would put lime into the water to kill any impurities so when you came out of the water you had two bloodshot eyes, as the lime irritated them. When I got home Aunt Kitty would shout at me.

"Were you at the baths?"

"No I was round at the playground" said I trying to put on a straight face.

"Look in the mirror at your eyes, they are all bloodshot" she would say.

My Aunt Kitty had the measure of me and our Hanna would burst out laughing because I was caught red handed.

I remember the old children's playground and I must admit we spent many enjoyable hours there but never on a Sunday. The city fathers or city bigots whatever way you care to look at it decided that the children of the Markets where not entitled to play on a Sunday so they locked up all the swings and the front gate and with no playing fields available you had to find other ways and means of entertaining yourself. I often wonder were there no bolt cutters of angle grinders available back then?

When I was about fourteen years of age my friends and I would take a dander up the road towards Saintfield at the top of the Ormeau Road. Situated at the top of the Ormeau Road was a large building called Nazareth Lodge which ran from the Ormeau to the Raven Hill Road This was a convent which housed orphans and children that were born out of wedlock. It has row upon row of windows and is surrounded by a large fifteen foot wall. Similar to what one would imagine in a Charles Dickens story, such as Oliver Twist. However what went on behind these walls was far more horrifying than anything that Dickens could conjure up. It later transpired that two of Ireland's most notorious paedophile priests used to visit this establishment on a regular basis and I guess these two weren't the only ones. Children in the care of this establishment were raped beaten and tortured. Both these priests are now dead and in the case of one of them Fr Brendan Smith, it was reported that he died of natural causes whilst in custody serving a prison sentence for his heinous crimes. However I feel justifiably sceptical about the official version of events, due to the fact that this most evil individual managed to destroy the image and reputation of the Southern Government and they were going to make damn sure that such a negative perception should not be repeated. Fr Smith's accomplice Fr Fortune committed suicide. I always remember our Hanna saying that they are a good sod in the ground. What these children suffered must have been horrific, childhoods lost forever. I hope now as the years have passed that these innocent victims get the justice and closure they both need and deserve.

Billy's Weekly Liar was a small magazine which came out on a weekly basis and was very popular. It was printed in the Sandy Row area and was just some local jargon and some smutty jokes but apart from that it was just harmless fun. The Catholic Church made sure it was banned as they had the power to censor all reading material, newspapers, books, magazines etc, which they disapproved of. Peaser Green was about twenty years old and stood about five foot ten inches tall and was built like a tank. He could throw a punch like a pro boxer. He lived with his parents, brothers and sisters in Keegan Street not far from Stewart Street. I remember when I was around fourteen years old, my mates at the time were Eddie Wiglibe, who we used to call him Eddie Wigwam, Alex Mc Christen, and Tom Fitzsimons. Peaser Green would get us to stand at the top of Keegan Street keeping watch for his mother or father as he read Billy's Weekly Liar. Chuck Conlon told me about a time when he and Spike McCormack were at the Curzon picture house at the top of the Ormeau Road. They were standing in the aisle next to the far wall as all the seating was occupied and because of this you waited your turn to get a seat when someone left it. This was the protocol in all cinemas when there was standing room only. Anyway on this occasion Chuck and Spike were standing along the wall with Peaser Green standing just behind them. Running down the walls from the roof to the floor were these large wings that sat out from the wall.

There was this guy standing a short distance behind Peaser who shouted.

"Get your fucking big head out of the way I can't see the film."

Peaser quickly turned around and said.

"Are you talking to me?"

"Yes you. There's no one else with a dome that size" the guy shouted.

With that Peaser took a charge at him knocking two or three people flying in the process. He threw a left hook at the guy's head and missed and took a large chunk of masonry out of one of the wing supports. Chuck said the guy bolted for the exit with Peaser in hot pursuit.

Chuck Conlon bumped into Peaser a few days later.

"Well did you catch the guy?" said Chuck.

"Catch him" Peaser said laughing.

"A fucking greyhound wouldn't have caught him."

I am seventy four years old now and remember sitting in the cinema in my younger days like it was only yesterday watching the old westerns. When the Indians would be attacking the wagon train and just closing in on the settlers, you would hear the distant sound of a bugle which could only mean one thing, the US Calvary was on its way. Everyone in the audience would cheer as the Indians galloped off. You could picture that happening now days. Then at the end of the picture everyone would clap. They used to show a funny picture before the main viewing, it was called Laurel and Hardy but we used to call them fat and skinny. Then there were the three stooges which basically consisted of three head cases slapping each other around. That's why they were given the genre name of slap stick comedy. Another favourite of mine was the Marks Brothers, this was a class act. Then there were the cartoons such as Tom and Jerry, even today we can still enjoy the humour in these comedies.

In the fifties the summers were hotter than they are now days. One summer I went round to Norton Street to see the mate wee Willie Mc Mullen. He lived with his mother, father, brothers Rab and John Joe and sisters Peggy and Eileen. His big brother John Joe was tall and lean and head and shoulders taller than wee Willie. On this particular night we were coming down the Ormeau Road from the Curzon and nearing the park, when someone in the crowd standing over at the chip shop shouted something derogatory over at wee Willie. Willie shouted something back and two or three of them ran over and started throwing punches. I grabbed Willie and pulled him away.

"I'll get our John Joe for you" shouted Willie.

"Aye go and get him and bring plenty of backings with you" came the reply.

So we made our way down the Ormeau Road to Norton Street and wee Willie opened the door and called his big brother John Joe out.

"What's up" he said.

"Them bastards up the Ormeau Road hit me for nothing I was just walking past minding my own business when I was set upon."

Well that was enough for big John Joe; who immediately ran in and got his coat. With his teeth gritted he asked us to show him where they were and of the three of us went in search for the boys that hit Willie.

Just as we drew level John Joe shouted to Willie

"Is that them?"

"Aye" replied Willie.

Just at that John Joe ploughed through the crowd and grabbed two by the neck and slammed them against the plate glass window of the chippie.

"Which one of you bastards hit our Willie" he shouted into their faces.

There were eight of them in total, all in their late teens and not one of them said a word. John Joe then let go of the two guys and stood back facing the crowd.

"Right I'll give you all a fair dig two at a time" said John Joe.

They all looked at one another but not a word was uttered. Looking back on it there is not a doubt in my mind that John Joe would have carried out his threat. Before he left, he put it to them that if any of them laid a hand on his wee brother Wille that he would be back and to make no mistake about that. Afterwards when wee Willie and I would go for a walk up the Ormeau past the chippie, the same crowd would be standing there and when we passed they would nod over at us and wee Willie would look at me with a smile on his face.

As I have stated earlier our home depended on a gas supply for cooking and lighting and possessed no electricity supply. I remember we had this radio which was powered by battery and I used to bring the battery up to the shop in Cromac Street to get it charged which would last us a week. We eventually received an electricity supply in the late forties, which made life a lot easier and got the electric radio in, so we had better sound and more stations. One day I was listening to the wireless as we called it then and there was a knock at the door. I opened it to find Spike Mc Cormack standing there.

"Are you coming out to play" said Spike.

"Na" Said I. "I'm staying in to listen to the wireless."

Every time I think back on this I burst out laughing, now days its, I am playing with my console, I phone, plays station, lap top or watching my 3d sixty inch flat screen television.

When I was a young child we never seemed to get bored. There was rope skipping, bumping marbles, hand ball, cycling and a game called rallyo. Rallyo involved two opposing sides, each with their own den. Each side had an equal number of runners and they would take it in turn to send a runner out. The runner would be given a count to one hundred and then someone from the opposing den would give chase and if he caught up with the runner he would spit over his head and shout rallyo. If a runner was caught he would then have to join the opposing den and the den with the most kids one. Some of the runners would jump on buses which made it nearly impossible to track them down and this game could go on for hours. The winners received an ice- lolly from Martha McGlades shop and when you hit the sack that night you went out like a light. All that running would stand me in good steed in later years as it would one day save my life.

Building your own guider with ball bearings was a big thing then. Chuck and Spike would build theirs and then give me a hand to build my one, we helped each other out then. Some of the guiders would have pram wheels on them. Frankie Doherty nick named Funko, lived up at the top of Staunton Street and he possessed a massive guider which he built with large lorry wheel bearings on the front and back. He chopped sticks, bundled them up together and then used his guider to transport them around the doors of the neighbourhood and sold them for fire wood. Funko was a good grafter as were his brothers Dan, Tommy, Willie, Bimbo and Christy, who was the youngest, most of them worked at Inglis bakery.

Chapter 5

Some Of The Shops And neighbours of the Market

In Stanfield Street running into Welsh Street facing Matt Dalton's shop and Tommy Callan's bar lived Mickey Flanigan. Mickey sold fruit and veg and he lived with his wife Frances and two daughters Dolly and Madeline. Mickey was a real character and a great worker and his wife Frances was a lovely woman as was his sister Nell Nolan who lived beside me in Staunton Street. Anchor Paddy Glennon lived next door to Mickey and two doors down from Anchor Paddy lived the Vernors whose son I worked with at Inglis bakery. The space between Tommy Callan's, Mickey Flanagan's house and Matt Daltons shop is where the annual bonfire was held, to commemorate the ascension off Our Lady into heaven. If you can get your head round that one, how were they so sure of the date? It was probably an ancient pagan festival day, as Christianity hijacked many pagan holidays to encourage people to break away from the old pagan rituals. It fizzled out over the years as people lost interest or maybe felt this wasn't an appropriate way to celebrate Our Lady and it was replaced with anti internment bonfires from the early seventies onwards. Imagine saying to young people today that we had a bonfire on the fifteenth of August to commemorate the ascension of Our Lady into heaven, they would think there was something wrong with your head. Anyhow we would start collecting from June right up until the fifteenth of August, then around nine thirty that night we would light the bonfire with wood, tyres and anything else that would burn. There would be singing, drinking, merry making and feasting and a real sense of community spirit. There would be pigs feet stuck on spears and then put on the bonfire as a treat for all those who had gathered. You don't believe this do you? I couldn't blame you I was only having a laugh about the pigs feet. The houses surrounding the bonfire were sometimes damaged due to the heat, the windows would crack and the paint on the sills and doors would bubble and crack.

Martha and Joe McGlades shop situated in Eliza Street facing St Coleman's school was were I got my first ice lolly and packet of potato crisps. It was just after the war and Joe used to make his own ice lollies. He had a large freezer that he kept in his house beside the shop and he sold everything that we needed for the house. Martha McGlade had time for everyone then, man, woman and child. She knew what brand of cigarettes most people would smoke and if a child were to ask her for a certain brand Martha would say

"No love I'm afraid your mammy and daddy don't smoke that brand."

McGlades shop was where I would get Aunt Kitty's five Woodbine or Park Drive. I remember a particular occasion when a mother sent her son round to the shop to get her ten Woodbine and instructed him that if they had no Woodbine that he was to bring her round anything, so he brought her back an apple cake, which he was running around wearing as a cap on his head a few minutes later.

McGlades shop would open from early in the morning till late at night and also if someone was short of money they would get their goods on tick and it would go down in the wee black book. Just after the Second World War, the shops that had been rationed began to fill up with sweets and chocolates to the delight of children of all ages. During the war you could not have acquired luxury goods such as sweets and a lot of the shops and houses made their own confectionary products, such as candy apples, haystacks made with cornflakes, chocolate toffee cigars and lucky dip bags. The sugar was rationed so it had to be brought up from the south of Ireland, it was better known then as the black market as the south was neutral during the war years and you had to smuggle the goods across the border. Other items available on the black market were ladies nylons and cigarettes, it seems laughable now but think about it, smuggling from one part of your own country to another part of it. Then there was Joe Donnelly's and Annie Ross's shops in Murphy Street, Murdoch's fruit and veg in Cromac Street, Joe's ice cream shop, Shannon's butchers and Jimmy Lundy's who sold electrical and household goods. This is where Aunt Kitty would buy our Christmas toys. McSherry's in Cromac Street sold cigarettes, tobacco, comics, magazines and newspapers. This was the kid's entertainment centre as there were no I phones or even televisions in those days and comics were our sole enjoyment.

McKnight and Gambles in Cromac Street is where we purchased our shoes, water boots and gutties better known today as plimsoles. We got all our winter and summer clothes at McKnight and Gambles and Aunt Kitty would have to bring her clothing coupons, as all goods were rationed during the war years. Aunt Kitty would get a cheque from one of the many finance companies in town and pay it of weekly. It was usually holiday times such as Easter and Christmas when Aunt Kitty would fit us out with our new clothes and foot ware. Then there was McKinney's in Cromac Street who sold poultry and fresh eggs. The pawn shop near McCauley Street was where the mothers pawned their husbands suits on a Monday and redeemed them on a Friday and let's not forget

Barr's the barbers which was near the Post Office at Cromac Square and Kearney's facing Eliza Street. Tucker would be cutting your hair and he would leave you sitting on the chair while he'd run over to the Tommy Rodgers bookies, as you do. Now you would eventually get your hair cut but only after Tucker got to check his horse results and if Tuckers horse got beat he would leave you with scissor marks on your head. Just joking here Tucker you always got a good hair cut at Kearney's barbers. All of these shops and bars in and around the Markets and the people who ran them down through the years were the backbone of our community.

Collins shop was at the top of our street facing Eliza street and it for the most part sold confectionary and cigarettes. Next door to the shop lived Lady Kane and her maid in a large house with eight bedrooms. Lady Kane was a wee frail woman in her late sixty's and sometimes when she would come to the door and it was stormy outside you would notice the she always kept her hand on her head. It was said that she wore a wig and her maid was also a wee small woman who always wore a frilly apron and had a feather duster in her hand. Aunt Kitty said she owned half the block. Further on up Eliza street on the same side you had Jack Doyle who was a very successful builder and had a yard in McCauley street and around a dozen men on his payroll. A couple of doors further up you had the Madines, Sheila the eldest daughter had long auburn hair and would have put you in mind of Maureen O'Hara the actress. Her brother Bobby was a champion swimmer but Spike the mate was to beat him in a two length race in the Ormeau baths. A few doors on up you had the

Magee's, her eldest son Patsy Geezer we would have called him, he was around my own age, medium height with dark swarthy skin and he had a terrible habit of biting his nails. He had them down to the bone most of the time. He worked on and off for Geordie Stow who had a scrap yard in Lagan street facing the children's play ground and the bus station.

Aunt Kitties husband Thomas died in the late forties. He was buried with the four wheel hearse that had a glass case allowing you to view the coffin with two black horses pulling it along. Aunt Kitties neighbours wee Maggie McMullen, Rosie Rafferty, Theresa McCormick, Lizzie Conlon, Mrs Valliday, Bella Stigles, Ginny Keys, Mary McMullen, her mother Fanny Mattchet, Lizzie Mc Conkey, Mary Mckay and Maggie Docherty to name but a few all chipped in to help her with the wake. They brought her tea, sugar, bread, milk, cheese and cooked meat. They helped to make sandwiches and tea for all the visitors calling to pay their respects. Working class people were like that back in those days; then they helped each other out. Very few had a roughness in those days meaning they had very little income but they did the best they could and when anyone was in trouble or died everyone rallied around.

Chapter 6

Dundrum School Trip

I can remember my school days when the teachers would take us to the cinema. We would be subjected to Macbeth by William Shakespeare, what a load of crap that was, it wasn't my cup of tea at all. I remember going to watch Scott of the Antarctic where this Englishman and his team set off on an expedition to conquer the South Pole. However they never made it there as they all froze to death in their tents en-route. Some of the rooms in our house felt like that in the winter you know.

I was around fourteen years old when St Coleman's school was making plans to take us on a fortnight's holiday to Dundrum. We were to be accommodated in what was now a disused army barracks where the sleeping quarters were comprised of tin Nissan huts. There were a few of us selected from each class including Spike and myself. Mr Smith who was nicknamed Smiker was the school master who would be taking care of us at the camp. Aunt Kitty was reluctant to let me go as she was so overprotective and would worry about me going away for two weeks but I eventually talked her around into letting me go. Dundrum is on the County Down coast at the foot of the Mourne Mountains and about seven miles from the seaside resort town of Newcastle. Back then it was a one horse town, with a row of shops along the seafront and I'm sure not much has changed. There is a large Norman castle which is lying in ruins and it's located about a mile from the village. The cinema was also a large Nissn hut and is still standing today and in use as a repair garage.

We all boarded the bus outside our school building and Aunt Kitty and Spike's mother Teresa were standing there watching us leave with tears in their eyes. As I recall it was a very hot and sunny day around the end of June as we pulled out from Eliza Street and we all couldn't wait to get to the seaside. As the bus drove up to the centre of the village we couldn't take our eyes of the water and all the boys on the bus just wanted to head down to the beach for a swim. However old Smikers was having none of it and wanted the bus to head for the old army camp, so he could get all our luggage unloaded and sort out the sleeping quarters.

The Nissan huts ran the length and breadth of the camp and we were allocated one of these huts. Spike and I were allocated the same hut, the beds were in rows on each side of the Nissan huts and we got our gear on the beds we wanted. Everyone had their own personal locker in which to place his belongings and once we had unpacked we got ready to head into the village. Mr Smith lined us up and proceeded to give us a lecture on safety and keeping out of trouble. He told us that no one was to go swimming unless he was present to oversee us.

"And you all know the penalty for breaking the rules" he said and he meant it alright.

He was up to the mark in keeping thirty teenage boys in check at this point. We all headed into the village, Aunt Kitty had given me two pound notes, which, in those days was not bad at all. The only things we were interested in buying then was sweets and lemonade and the first shop we piled into was a chemist shop. Spike and I were at the back of the shop, while Bap Friel, Eddie Grey, big Hen Murphy and big Eddie Cooper to name but a few were at the front by the counter and there was also a local guy with a big Alsatian dog standing at the counter. Somebody from our crowd bought a packet of lozenges but there was so many of us in there that you couldn't get near the counter. So we all piled out of the shop and onto the street and there was nothing left in the shop which was packed with stuff such as tooth brushes, toothpaste, lozenges and other items before we entered. We all then headed for a walk along the beach, the tide was in and we were skimming flat stones across the water to see who could shoot the furthest. We stayed at the beach skimming for a couple of hours which was great craic and then we headed back to the camp as it was almost supper time.

We went down to the canteen which was situated in one of the Nissan huts and was staffed by a couple of local women. After a feed of chips, sausages and beans we went outside to play on an old cabin cruiser that was laying abandoned in the barracks complex. Jimmy Kennedy, Tommy McCormack and the two Doherty brothers Tommy and John (who I still have the odd pint with, especially when I'm buying, just joking John) where all there and would team up with Spike and I to go exploring. We headed over to the old Norman castle, which was not far from the camp to explore the old ruins. The large stones that had fallen from its walls over the years littered the surrounding area but it must have been some castle in its day. We walked around the walls to take in the size of the place, it was rather extensive and we didn't realize the time until someone looked at their watch and seen that it was already nine thirty. It was still bright but we had to be back in the camp for ten but it was only a ten minute walk back to the camp. Mr Smith took a head count to make sure no one was missing, we had a wash then had a hot drink and some sandwiches then got ready for bed and once I hit the sack I was out for the count.

Next morning, a Sunday, Mr Smith woke us at seven o'clock to get ready for mass, something I wasn't looking forward to, come to think of about it nobody was but Mr Smith made sure everyone attended to their good Catholic duties. He decided that we should go to chapel first and then get the breakfast when we returned to camp. Back then you had to fast before you could receive communion anyway, so we were all seated waiting for the priest to begin mass, when Spike, who was seated beside me collapsed in his seat. Mr Smith ran down the aisle to lift Spike and get him outside for some fresh air. Then another one fell and another one and in the end I counted eight in all had fallen. Eddie Gray, Bap Friel and big Hen Murphy ran down the aisle to give Mr Smith a hand with lifting the boys outside. Spike was something else to lift as he was very well built for his age but they managed to get him out into the air. Big Henry Murphy came out with a jug of water and I believe it must have been holy water because when they had all taken a drink and began to recover and feel a bit better and most of them wanted to go back into mass, just having a laugh here! Mr Smith decided to get back to camp as soon as possible and get the lads their breakfast and we were all glad to hear that as we didn't want to sit and listen to a boring sermon for an hour or so, what child would? Well not this child anyhow.

When we returned to the camp we had our breakfast which was the breakfast of kings, sausages, bacon, eggs and toast. After we finished, we headed out to play and walked out to the parade ground as the British Army would have called it, only to find Mr Smith standing there with the local man I'd seen in the chemist shop the previous day by his side. The man still had his fully grown Alsatian dog with him. Mr Smith lined us up on the parade ground and explained to us what happened in the chemist shop the day before about the goods that went missing from the counter. He said that he would really appreciate it if the goods were returned. No one said a word.

"Whoever took the goods would they please step forward" said Mr Smith.

He repeated his request and when he didn't get any reply he approached the local guy and asked him to pick out the boys that he had seen stealing the goods. The local guy, who was around eighteen years old walked down the line with his Alsatian dog picking out the culprits that he said had taken the goods. Each one that he picked out was totally in denial of any wrong doing. Mr Smith then thanked the local guy and he took the boys who were picked out to the side and had a stern talk with them. He then informed them that they were grounded and were not to leave the camp until such a time as the missing goods were returned. The next day the goods that had gone missing were left in Mr Smith's living quarters and were subsequently returned to the chemist shop and looking back on it I would put it down to a school boy prank nothing that serious.

A few days later, a few of the boys including big Henry Murphy, Bap Friel and Eddie Gray were down in the village when they ran into the local guy with the Alsatian dog. He shouted something over at them and that was enough for the lads who rushed over and proceeded to give both him and his dog a good tanking and the poor dog was never seen again.

At bed time we used to partake in pillow fights, in which each hut would challenge the other, it was all good fun as you couldn't do much damage with a pillow, unless you were to put a couple of bricks in it I guess. One day a guy came into our hut and informed us that we were going to the picture house to see Ting Tong (he couldn't pronounce his k's) so that night we all headed down to the cinema with Mr Smith leading the way. The large Nissan hut had ample seating and could seat around one hundred and fifty, which was great and we were all seated comfortably with our sweets and lemonade. It was time for lights out and the wee show came on first. The wee show was Laurel and Hardy which we thoroughly enjoyed as the roars of laughter could be heard outside the hut. Laurel and Hardy were followed by Tom and Jerry and then came the main event. In the film staring Fey Wray and Robert Armstrong, a film crew land on an island to search for a giant ape named King Kong. I don't know who played the part of Ting Tong because he must have been one large lad.

The natives capture Fey Wray (the girl) and tie her up waiting for the arrival of King Kong who is the size of a ten story building. After snatching the girl King

Kong headed off through the jungle to his lair with the film crew in hot pursuit. Half way through the picture King Kong gets into a scrap with a T-Rex who was attempting to steal his girl, wrong move mate. King Kong then sets about kicking the shit out of the big T-Rex and ends up breaking its jaw, grabs the girl and bolts for his den deep in the jungle. The film crew eventually capture King Kong by rendering him unconscious with gas bombs and transporting him to New York where they put him on display while he is held in chains. He eventually escaped from captivity, causing havoc and grabbing the girl before heading for the Empire State Building and climbing to the top of it. Within minutes the government scramble a number of airplanes that proceed to attack King Kong and shoot him down but just before he falls he lays wee Fay Wray down out of harms way. You could call it a beauty and the beast story. So on his way down from the top of the Empire State which is about three quarters of a mile drop, Ting Tong's life is flashing before him as he is thinking to himself how the fuck did I end up here in this God forsaken place. I was quite happy running around the jungle grabbing a couple of wee maidens, tickling their bellies and beating the fuck out of the odd T-Rex having a rare old time to myself, instead of chasing wee Fay Wray half way round the world but I guess that's what happens when you fall in love. It was curtains for poor old Ting Tong.

The question going the rounds in the camp the next day was what are eighteen pounds each and we would reply was that's what King Kong's balls weigh, laughing our heads off. Mr Smith also took us on a day trip into Newcastle which was a couple of miles down the road from Dundrum where we spent some time on the beach collecting crabs williks and shells. There was also an amusement arcade and dodgem cars, merry go rounds and we had great craic there. The weather held out the whole time we were in Dundrum and the two weeks flew in and it wasn't long before we were back home in the Markets. Aunt Kitty was certainly glad to see me and she had a large pot of ribs cooking on the stove that you could smell half way down the street and I polished of a plate of them in no time.

.

Chapter 7

Defying The Ivy Gang And A Cycle To Dundalk

One Sunday morning when I believe I was around seventeen years of age at the time, it was a fine summer's morning and Aunt Kitty was frying breakfast and our Hanna was doing the ironing.

"I'm going for a spin on the bike up to the Ormeau Park." I said to Aunt Kitty.

"Don't forget to be in for you're Sunday dinner at four o'clock" she shouted back from the working kitchen.

Aunt Kitty always expected you to be in on time when she was giving out the dinner out and there was no microwave ovens back then to heat up your food. Wee Willy McMullan was standing at his front door in Norton street smoking as I cycled up the street.

"Want to take a spin up to the park?" I said.

"Right I'll get my bike" replied Willy.

We made our way up to the Ormeau Embankment and headed for the middle gate of the park. In the middle of the park, one end stretched out towards the Ravenhill Road and this is where the local loyalist Ivy Gang would hang about. There were usually around a couple of hundred of them and they would attack Catholics when the opportunity arose which was quite often especially when you were on your own or with your girl coming out of the pictures. They liked to hang around in large numbers because that way they felt safe and anyone from the Markets who would be unfortunate to come across them could expect a beating. Willy and I were standing having a smoke as I looked towards the Ravenhill Road and I could see this large crowd of fellas of in the distance wearing their long Teddy boy coats heading in our direction.

"If I'm not mistaken Willy I think that's the Ivy Gang" I said.

"Stand your ground" Willy said.

Now if I had any sense or the brain I was born with I should have been cycling down Eliza Street as soon as he mentioned the word ground but I wasn't going to leave him on his own. This may sound like John Wayne talk here as there were around twenty five of them and that's not bad odds, considering there were only two of us, just having a laugh here. As they drew closer I could see that they were led by this small ginger haired git called Alexander who was about the same size as wee Willy and this Alexander guy seemed to be giving the orders as they surrounded and encircled us. I don't know what it was about Wee Willy but he seemed to attract gangs like a fucking magnet. They opened their coats to reveal their studded belts and I was wearing a snake belt around my waist at the time, not much good here I thought to myself. At that moment and as calm as you like wee Willy walked towards this Alexander character and says to him.

"A fair go you and me"

I could see that Alexander was getting agitated and nervous probably thinking to himself, if this wee man gives me a tanking I'll lose face with my gang and he was looking for a way out and his opportunity arose when he spotted this guy sitting on one of the park benches with an Alsatian dog.

"I think that guy's a detective and he's been watching us since we entered the park" said Alexander to his mates.

Now this guy no more looked like a detective than the man in the moon, he had a wee skinny head and I'm sure you'll agree with me when I say that most cops that you and I have seen possess these big large domes.

Alexander turned to his associates saying

"Let's go lads we'll get them again" and with that they headed off.

"Not if I can fucking help it" I muttered to myself.

"Right Willy let's get the fuck out of here in case they change their mind" I said and with that we cycled out of the park and down the Ormeau Road lucky to get out all in one piece.

This same Ivy Gang would on occasion come down to Alfred Street which was in the Markets to sign on the dole and Terry McCartan and Charlie Harmon would often pull them out of the queue and give them a digging.

Davy Rock was known as a local hard man and he certainly looked the part. I remember one night when Dee Dee Conlon and I were waiting to get the bus up the Ormeau to the picture house when along came Davy Rock. I was around fifteen years old at the time and Dee Dee was a year or so older than me. Davy Rock was half cut as he approached us and stopped looking down at Dee Dee.

"How much have you?" he said to Dee Dee.

"Three and six to get the bus and pay into the pictures" said Dee Dee.

"Hand it over" Davy snarled at him.

"No, I need it" replied Dee Dee and with that Rock grabbed him by the lapels and lifted him up to eye level.

"If you were my size I would knock your bollocks in" said Rock before lowering him and staggering off. Fast forward a few years when the troubles broke out and Dee Dee was to get his revenge. Davy Rock was standing in Mick Moonies in Cromac Street drinking at the bar when Dee Dee came in with a few mates, spotted Rock and called him over.

"Get into that cubicle, I want to have a word with you" said Dee Dee.

"Did you pull my mate Spike McCormack? Asked Dee Dee.

"It was only a wind up Dee Dee" replied Rock.

"You ever lay a hand on Spike and you'll answer to me" said Dee Dee.

Now man to man Davy Rock would have torn Dee Dee apart but he wasn't going to chance it as at the time Dee Dee had an equalizer up his coat and with that Rock got up without saying a word and headed for the door. After the Ormeau Park fiasco Davy Rock got a gang together in the Markets and marched up the Ormeau road and around the embankment towards the Ravenhill Road right into the heart of the Ivy Gang's territory. There were a few members of the Ivy Gang hanging about the corners but they scattered when they saw the gang from the Markets heading towards them. After that they just seemed to fade away and nothing more was heard from them, or maybe Alexander feared another stand off with Wee Willy, who knows.

The Wolftone Band from the Markets ran a bus to Dundalk in the fifties, our mate Charlie Conlon played the bagpipes and Paddy McMahon from Carrick Hill, the Iron Man we nicknamed him was the drum major. The band was run by Ted McMullen out of Welsh Street and it the only republican band to ever march up Royal Avenue in the early fifties and the police Chief who gave the go ahead for it was sacked. Davey Moss, Bo Bobbie McAlvenny and his brother Paddy, Jim Gaohen and big Tommy McGahan were some of the men travelling in the bus but my mates and I decided to cycle down to Dundalk. I was around seventeen at the time and Eddie Wigwam, Wee Willy McMullan, Jackie Scott and Eddie Meehan cycled with me. It was a bit of a gallop you might say but we were young and fit and to cycle that distance and back shouldn't pose any problem and let's just say it sounded good on paper.

We took all the necessary cooking utensils with us plus the eggs, bacon, sausages, sandwiches and flasks of tea. That Sunday morning I got up at five am crept down stairs as I didn't want to waken Aunt Kitty as she thought I was going on the bus and she would have worried about me cycling all the way to Dundalk. I brought the bicycle outside and it was starting to brighten up as it was the middle of May. As I made my way round to Meehan's house he was already cycling down Stanfield Street. We then gathered up the rest of the lads and headed for the Lisburn Road. As we got up as far as the King's Hall someone suggested that we stop and have a mug of tea so we all pulled up parked our bikes and got the flasks and sandwiches out.

"At this fucking rate we'll arrive in Dundalk sometime next week" I said.

We headed towards Lisburn and out into the country and after about five mile on we stopped again for more tea and sandwiches before heading on towards Newry, a bit of a gallop to go yet. We eventually came to a field which had a river running down from the mountains so we stopped to heat up some water for our flasks. Somebody had a pot and Jackie Scott said we should go and seek out a potato field, so he cycled up the road and came back a half an hour later with a sack full of spuds. Someone asked him how he knew it was a potato field and Jackie who was always good for a laugh replied.

"There was this big sign in the middle of the field which read free potatoes are growing in this field take all you want"

We soon got the spuds that Jackie had so kindly collected for us into the pot and placed it on the primer stove and boiled them up. We fried up the sausage, bacon and egg and got tucked in. Not before long we were on the road again and heading towards Newry.

Every steep hill we came to would prompt me to mutter to myself.

"Why the fuck didn't I get the bus."

Some would get off their bikes and walk up as it was pretty hard going. It was about twelve mid day by the time we arrived in Newry, so we headed for the nearest café where we guzzled down milkshakes, a far cry from the pints of porter we would neck in later years. We got cleaned up at the bus station before continuing on to Dundalk and we made it in good time too, as it was downhill for the most part. It had been overcast all day and it wasn't long before it started to rain, it was a blessing it wasn't heavy as we had no raincoats and nowhere to shelter but thank God it didn't last for long. The sun was coming out again as we cycled into Dundalk where the band had already arrived. They were all in the bar having a drink before the march and some of our lads decided it would be a good time to join them. My front tyre was going flat so I got the puncture outfit out and fixed the tube. Chuck and the rest of the Wolf Tone Band emerged from the bar and set about tuning up their bagpipes, Jesus what a racket they made, it sounded like someone was pulling cats tails. They formed onto the road and marched down the main street with us walking on the footpath. The town was filled with crowds by now and I have to say the band looked the part that day. With their banners flying and their pipes and drums keeping in tune playing

"They keep our lads in English jails" and "God save Ireland cried the hero's."

We hung about the town for a while before deciding to head for home.

We were cycling out of town when all of a sudden Jackie Scott's bike hit a pothole and buckled his front wheel. His bike was a top of the range racer, light as a feather and he attempted to straighten the wheel so he could ride it home but to no avail. We went back with him to see if he could get on the band's bus and when we got that sorted we then all headed for home with me having to steer Jackie's bike with one hand and my own with the other. We stopped a few miles up the road and had a smoke.

"I think we should get the bus" said Eddie Wigwam and we were all in agreement especially myself as I had two bikes to take home.

"Has anyone got the fare?" Asked Wee Willy but we only had about one pound fifty between us.

"That's no good we'll need more than that" said I.

Meehan said we could ask the driver as he had heard somewhere before that you could offer to put your name and address in a book and offer to pay later, so we made our way into Newry and headed for the bus station. Meehan went up and spoke to one of the drivers who agreed to let us ride home if we agreed to pay the bill by the end of the week, which we agreed to before putting our bikes in the luggage compartment. We headed home and I fell asleep as soon as I sat down on the bus. Two weeks later we all got a bill from Ulster Bus which we still haven't paid to this day and that was more than fifty years ago, the interest must run in to the hundreds.

Thank God it wasn't Beanie Beattie we owed it too. Oh nave I not told you about Beanie yet? Keep reading I will.

Chapter 8

Coming Of Age And The Pubs Are A Beckoning

My uncle Robert Robinson who was my mother's brother who was de mobbed fromthe army, came to live with Aunt Kitty for a few years. He was employed in Inglis bakery as a lorry driver. Robert stood five feet ten inches tall, was stoutly built and was always joking and laughing. On a Saturday night he would have a drink in Tommy Callens bar. He was generally joined by his two mates, my uncle Joe Hinds who was married to my Aunt Kathleen, my mother's sister and Dominic Donnelly our Roberts mate from Varner Street in the Falls district.

Aunt Kitty would put a large pot of ribs and onions on the stove and cook them up for Robert and his mates coming home from the bar.

After a good drinking session there is nothing better than to get stuck into a plate of freshly cooked pork ribs. Uncle Joe who was de mobbed from the air force would often do his party piece for anyone he thought he could entertain. He would put a towel around his head and with a basin turned upside down and his face blackened with soot beat the bottom of the basin and sing like an Indian faker. He was great craic and our Hanna and Aunt Kitty were in stitches laughing at him. Our Robert had three children two sons young Robert and Blue and a daughter called Alana and thankfully I have met them on occasion from time to time.

Friday and Saturday nights were gargle nights around the Markets and with the amount of pubs in the vicinity we were spoilt for choice. Every corner you turned there was a couple of bars but this wasn't a result of the Markets people being such heavy drinkers, far from it.

These pubs would accommodate the large influx of people from all over the country on market day. Farmers, travelling people, horse traders, fruit and veg men, fish mongers and livestock dealers would all gather in May's Market each and every Friday. The bars I remember were Barney McCoy's and Melees in Cromac Square, McIntees on the corner of Henrietta Street, the Golden Jubliee, Sil McGuire's, Donnelly's beside the wee church, McGuiness in May Street, the Royal Bar facing the fruit market, Hans Savages sounds like a German name in Annette Street facing the bus station, Billy Edges Lagan Street, Tommy Callans Welsh Street, Malachy Kerr's Eliza Street, Tom McGorans Stanfield Street facing Henderson's engineering works, Mick Moonies in Eliza Street, the Bulls Head in Cromac Street, Divines in McCauley Street and the Black Bull in Cromac Square; plenty to pick from and I hope I haven't left any out. Then there was also the other popular vice which was betting and the bookies shops or get rich quick centres as I like to call them were also in abundance in and around the Markets. There was Tommy Rodgers in Cromac Street beside Mick Moonies pub and crying Al McMurry's beside Lagan Lane. If you touched for a bet in Crying Al's, which was a rare occasion indeed, he would whine

"How did you touch for that one" he would say.

Then you had Docherty's in Market Street where the bookie who owned it before Doherty done a runner. There was a horse that won the Grand National at a big price of twenty to one. Nearly everyone in the Markets backed it and he couldn't pay out so he put a sign in the window which read when the fields are white with daisy's I'll return. Well at least he was honest about it. Then you had Duffs in McCauley Street and Shankers on Annette Street which was beside the Royal Bar.

At that time I would speculate that seven out of ten men in the Markets would have had a bet at some time in their lives. Even when you were at school you would on occasion have a bet at dinner time and when you finished school would nip round to see the race results. I can't speak for everyone but this gambling compulsion would stay with me for the rest of my life but it was all we had back then. One Saturday afternoon Spike McCormack and I were in Billy Edges pub in Lagan Street watching the racing on TV. Sammy Smiley the barman gave Spike a sheet of paper.

"Do that bet for me" and with that he handed Spike a ten pence piece.

"What's this for" said Spike.

"Do me a ten pence fourteen timer."

I burst out laughing because I knew Sammy was winding Spike up.

"Are you sure you have enough horses wrote down there Sammy" said I.

Spike rolled the piece of paper up and thumbed it across the bar.

"Fuck off Sammy" said Spike laughing.

Eddie Meehan and I would do our bets at Doherty's in Market Street. Eddie just lived down the street from me, a few doors from Silver McKee. Eddies circumstances were almost similar to mine as his mother had died young and his father remarried and left Eddie and his sister Mary to be reared by their grandfather Johnny Lowe. Johnny's wife passed away and it was no easy task to undertake bringing up your two grandchildren after rearing your own family. His daughter Alice Archer and her family lived a few doors down from him so I guess that was a help. Meehan and I backed this horse one day; the papers said it was a good thing. How many times down through the years, have I heard that Statement. After backing the horse Eddie and I dandered up to his grandfathers house to watch the race on TV. Old Johnny was sitting in his armchair watching the racing and although Johnny didn't gamble he still liked watching the racing on TV and his old eyesight was failing him as he was in his seventies. His son John was also there. He was nicknamed Pigeon and he was a heavy punter.

"I hope I'm on a few pints if this horse wins" he says to his nephew

Old Johnny picked out a grey horse to cheer for and I believe it was the only one he could make out on the TV. After Old Johnny picked the grey John the son shouted over.

"Dan, tear that docket up its no chance."

I wasn't too worried about Old Johnny's selection as it was running in last place.

"There's a bit to go yet and we are looking good" said I.

As the horses were coming to the last fence, ours was in front but the grey was making steady progress from the back of the pack and eventually drew level with ours. Over the last fence ours crashed on landing leaving the grey well clear. Old Johnny was cheering the grey horse on all the way until it crossed the finish line a winner at odds of ten to one.

"How much did you win" said Eddie to Old Johnny.

"Nothing, I never backed it" replied Old Johnny.

"While you were cheering on that grey big Dan and I were losing a right few quid on that favourite" said Eddie

"Well son that's not my problem and maybe that's why you and big Dan never have any money" Old Johnny shouted back at him.

He couldn't have said a truer word I thought to myself.

Now days gambling has taken on a whole new meaning, you can bet twenty four seven at any time of the day or night anywhere in the world.

With your I phone, laptop and computer you can even play the role of the bookie and lay the favourite to get beat but you need a healthy bank balance. There is even cartoon racing now. Jesus Christ they will stop at nothing to get money of the poor punter now days and some guys actually take this cartoon racing seriously. I can recall an occasion when I overheard this guy telling his mate after one of these races.

"Another furlong and my horse would have won."

My God I thought to myself, they say a horses brain [not the cartoon horses] is the size of a pea, well this guys must have been the size of a pin head. The winner was Mickey Mouse, Pluto was second and Daffy Duck came third, my God has it really come to this.

There were three hide and skin stores in and around the Markets. They were in Eliza Street, Welsh Street and Lagan Street. People coming to visit the Markets would hold their noses passing these stores. The cow hides would be transported from the abattoir which was situated in Stewart Street. The store workers would lay these hides out on the floor, trim them, cut the hoofs or hocks off, spread rock salt on them which would cure the hides and then they would be ready to be made into leather. Two men I knew personally big Henry Murphy and big Joe Rafferty would push these carts that were full of blood soaked hides weighing up to two hundred weight or more down from the abattoir.

You had to be big and strong to push these carts up and down Stanfield Street to the hide and skin stores. In rain, hail sleet and snow these men stepped up to the mark. They wore large rubber aprons down to their rubber boots and the carts were caked in blood which leaked on to the road. In the summer the flies would swarm in their millions on to Stanfield Street to feed off the iron in the blood. People in the Short Strand used to comment how they never seen a fly during the hot summer days and not a bit of wonder because the flies were all down the Markets getting well fed on the cows blood. When they were finished for the day and I mean the workers and not the flies, the streets would be washed down with a large water hose and it was the same when the cows would emerge from the large gateway in Robinson's cattle yard in Upper Stanfield Street. The cows would make their way up to the abattoir and the cows dung would clutter the streets and footpaths.

Big Joe Rafferty lived facing me in Staunton Street with his mother Rose and father Joe Senior. One day Big Joe was making his way down Stanfield Street with a load of hides from the abattoir and I was heading up to Matt Dalton's shop in Welsh Street for cigs, as big Joe drew the cart level I said.

"How's things big Joe."

He dropped the cart on it's two back legs and placing his left leg on the cart and smiling he said. "What are you after Dan?"

"Where did you get that idea from Big Joe?" I replied. "But since you brought it up could you get me three sirloins?"

"Dan it's like trying to get gold bars out of Fort Knox" said Joe.

"I'll take a few of those to" said I laughing.

"I'll see what I can do" replied Joe.

"Cut the fat of them" I said.

As usual and always quick with an answer he replied "Would you like me to cook them for you to?"

"Aye would you Joe" I said kidding.

"I'd like them medium rare with tomatoes and mushrooms."

I'll not tell you what he said after that but I told him I would leave him a couple of pints behind the bar in Tommy Callen's.

"Big Dan If I lined up all the pints I was promised and never got I wouldn't have to buy another pint for the rest of my life" replied Joe.

With that he lifted up his cart full of hides like it was a Dinky toy and strolled off. In saying that I did get my sirloins and I left big Joe his pints and money for a bet and I hope the bet touched Big Joe.

The Markets used to have a reputation for producing hard fighting men. One of the reasons for this was Ma Copley's boxing booth which was situated in the chapel fields around St Malachy's chapel. People came from all over Ireland, England, Scotland and Wales to compete at this venue. This was in the early thirties a bit before my time, well maybe not that much. Some of my present drinking buddies in the City Hibernians club are Brian McStravick, big Leo Davis my brother in law, Tony Lynch my son in law and Shaun Russell. Shaunie was a first class amateur boxer who could fight inside the ring as well as out. He broke his hand on some poor guy's head which was a pity as he was certainly Olympic material at the time. Brian keeps winding Shaunie up and just the other day as they were walking home, Shaunie was wearing his leather coat and Brian says to him.

"Hey, Shaunie they are not making them leather coats anymore."

"Why not?" Wee Shaunie replied.

"Because they ran out of plastic cows" said Brian.

Shaunie's brother Hughie won a bronze medal at the commonwealth games and Brian McStravick's father

Terry who was from the New Lodge he used to box at the chapel fields, and his first purse was five shillings. That was big money in those days as you could have bought a house for twenty quid, ok so it wasn't a mansion but now days you couldn't buy a doll's house for twenty quid. Terry who was a great boxer in his day defeated three British champions in non title fights but Brian said he hated fighting and wouldn't let any of his sons take up boxing. Terry's eldest son who is also called Terry, now lives believe it or not in a fold facing where the old chapel fields used to be…It's a small world alright.

Then there were also the McStravicks who lived in Annette Street I don't think they were related, Bucko and his clan. The two nephews, Shaunie and Pat whom I would see from time to time in the City Hibs Club, where we would partake in a pint or three. Pat is a fair snooker and darts player and a wee gentleman at that. Back in the day we would head for the Plaza dance hall and would start off drinking in Wee Billy Edge's in Lagan Street and would end up in the Garrick bar in Chichester Street. There would be Spike McCormack, Chuck Conlon and myself and on the odd occasion Larry McGuinness who lived in Stanfield Street would join us. As you know the rule of thumb where there is a company of drinkers there is a round system. Each person would honour his round of drinks, so this one night Larry declared his hand right away that he never had any wages to lift that week as he was on the sick.

"That's ok you don't have to worry about money you are in good company" said Chuck.

As the evening wore on and we were beginning to feel the effects of the beer we decided to head up to the Plaza dance hall which was just down the street as the ladies would be wondering what was keeping us. When we got to the front doors I asked.

"Has anyone got any tickets to save us paying in."

At that moment Larry put his hand in his top pocket.

"I have tickets" at which time he pulled out this large white fiver.

"Jesus H Christ where did that come from" said Spike.

"I forgot I had it in my top pocket" Larry muttered feeling rather embarrassed.

"Right lets head back to the Garrick and continue where we left off and Larry's buying till closing time.

We never made it back to the Plaza that night as the doors closed at eleven and I staggered round home to Aunt Kitty's feeling worse for wear. My head hit the pillow and I was out for the count and no wonder since I was awake from five that morning to cover my shift in Inglis bakery and I guess the clatter of pints may also have contributed to it. When I awoke that Saturday morning I was suffering from a massive hangover and was thinking to myself I wish to fuck Larry had never pulled that white fiver out.

Paddy McKee better known as Silver was born in Market Street just off Cromac Square to Maggie and Paddy McKee, he was around five feet ten tall, of stocky build and possessed hands like two ham shanks and was as strong as a bull. He was employed by Allams stock yard as a cattle drover. In the winter he always wore his fawn crombi overcoat, shirt and tie and his famous brown boots. Silver was a colourful character and was known as a man to be handy with his fists the length and breadth of Ireland. I recall sitting across from him at a card table in the Nortonville Billiards Club above Tommy Callens Bar in Stanfield Street. Cliff Richard was performing his number one hit Living Doll on the television and sitting beside me was young Joe Dorian and big Bobby Murphy. We were having a game of scotch seven card with jokers wild at five shillings a man. I was winning a couple of hands as was young Joe and big Bobby but Silver McKee was on a losing streak and not in the best of moods when some fella walked in the door. This guy was tall and heavy set and was half cut and he made his way over to our table and struck up a conversation with young Joe Dorian. At that Silver roared.

"Fuck off wee lad cant you see we are trying to have a game of cards here."

"I am not talking to you" the guy said turning to McKee and at that Silver gave him a back hander that landed him across the floor on to his back. Young Joe ran over and lifted the guy to his feet.

"There was no call for that" young Joe shouted over to McKee who without saying a word turned to his game of cards not wanting it seemed to me , to tangle with young Joe who helped the guy down the stairs. From that day on I put Silver down as a bully.

I remember a certain occasion when this fellow was giving his wife a hard time, he was shouting and yelling and wrecking the house which was opposite Silvers house. Maggie silvers mother asked him to intervene, so Silver took a stroll across the street and rapped the door. When the guy opened the door McKee addressed him saying.

"Knock that in the head wee lad."

"Fuck off and mind your own business" replied the guy and with that McKee whacked him leaving him in a heap at his feet and with a broken jaw which meant eating out of a straw for six weeks.

I seen Silver giving Davy Rock a tanking in Murphy Street and every time Silver would knock him down Rock would bounce back up again, for there was no fear in Davy. Then the RUC about ten in number came on the scene and broke up the fight and at that both McKee and Rock got stuck into the cops and it developed into a full scale riot as some of the men standing around watching the fight became involved. Big Paddy Rafferty, Hoot Gibson, Pronto Conlon, Billy Lagan, Tucker McCalister, Gerry Maxwell, Sugar Robinson, big Freddie Webb, Gerry Reynolds and young Joe Dorian but to name a few. The RUC withdrew from the area and a few weeks later Silver was arrested and eventually ended up serving a three month jail term for disorderly behaviour. I would sometimes ring Chuck Conlon to get the names of certain characters as I would forget and Chuck has a good memory for dates and places, he now lives in Turf Lodge. Not far from Chuck lives big Billy Bright a Market man and one of natures gentlemen.

Chapter 9

Beannie Beattie And Maggie Elder

Directly facing our house in Staunton Street stood Bennie Beatties shop at the corner of Keegen Street. Bennies married name was Morgan. She was married to Dan Morgan who worked in the abattoir. Bennie was of medium height, stoutly built and had dark swarthy skin although she was most recognizable by her three gold teeth when she smiled. Though she didn't smile very often, only when she was getting paid back what she was owed, for Bennie was a money lender. Aunt Kitty informed me that in the thirties Bennie would hire shawls, pots and pans and she charged five shillings in the pound. Refusing to honour your commitments to Bennie was not an option for the term 'hell hath no fury like a woman scorned' originated with Bennie. Bennie was a money lender, debt collector and enforcer all rolled in to one. She would stand at her door with arms folded constantly on the look out for any poor unfortunate who was late with their payment. On her fingers she had three or maybe four gold and diamond rings that originally belonged to the poor unfortunate people who owed her money and were unable to redeem them. If she spotted someone who defaulted on a loan she would let out a roar that froze the victim in his or her tracks like a rabbit caught in the head lights of a car.

Charlie Conlon 'Chuck' as we called him lived a couple of doors up from our house with his mother Lizzie. He had two brothers called John Dee and Eddie. Patsy McCormack who was nicknamed 'Spike' lived in Campbell's Place a cul-de-sac next to our house. He lived there with his mother Theresa, father Arthur, brothers John and Tommy and sister Mary. The three of us would have a few jars together at the weekend; in fact it was quite a few. One Thursday Chuck decided to ask Bennie for a loan to go out that weekend as he only had a couple of days work in the bakery that week. He asked Bennie for a loan of six pounds, twenty five which incurred one pound and five shillings of interest weekly. If you could not repay the loan in full by the end of the week you were required to pay the weekly interest, which for example could amount to sixty five pounds over a full year. Many a one had to pay the interest as they could not afford to pay the full loan but that suited Bennie for that was twelve times the loans worth and she was still owed the original fiver. Chuck came out of Bennie's shop with his big white fiver. A fiver then in the fifties would be equivalent to about a hundred and fifty pounds or more now day's. I reminded Chuck that he better not default on his loan because we all know what Bennies like.

"I'll pay her weekly." He said smiling, very weakly he meant. I told him I would bring him the daily newspapers up to the hospital as that's where she would put him. I laughed and stated that it was also my intention to go see Bennie on Saturday to get my own loan. This would take me out for the weekend as I had only gotten one day's work in English's bakery that week and after giving Aunt Kitty my keep I was left with very little. However not to worry I thought I'll have my big white fiver tomorrow. I retired early that Friday night and come Saturday morning I arose as usual and came downstairs for my breakfast. Aunt Kitty was in the scullery frying bacon when she suddenly announced.

"Bennie Beattie died last night"

My jaw just dropped. Jesus Christ I thought to myself there goes my weekend but I knew there would be some happy faces around the Markets after hearing of Bennie's demise and none would be happier than Chuck Conlon. Jack Beattie Bennies brother later declared that anyone who owed Bennie money could forget about paying it back. Little did he realize they already had that in mind as soon as they received the sad or maybe not so sad news of Bennie's passing especially if you were one of those that had borrowed a rather large loan.

The bars around the Markets were crowded that night and I wonder why?

I met Spike McCormack that morning.

"Did you hear about Bennie?" I asked him.

"Don't talk to me. I just paid my loan out last week and was going for another one next Saturday. You would think she might have waited another week before dying on us."

Maggie Elder better known as Maggie Conlon lived at the corner shop between Murphy Street and Stanfield Street. On Friday and Saturday nights she would boil up cow's elders known as adders and pigs feet. You had to boil them up for hours in order to soften them and make them easy to slice. When we would get kicked out of the pubs at closing time which was around ten thirty we would head round to Maggie Elders but Friday was a fast day and you ate only fish so Maggie Elders was out of bounds. The alter rail eaters would all gather outside Joe Donnelly's shop facing Maggie's waiting on Maggie to give the go ahead.

"They will be ready in ten minutes" she would shout. When they were ready everyone would rush over to get their order in.

Buckie Lagan, the brother of Eddie Lagan would usually be the first in line.

"A couple of slices of elder and two pig's feet" he would shout.

"That will be one shilling and sixpence" Maggie would reply.

Thomas McConkey nick named Monty would also be in the queue. He lived beside me in Staunton Street with his parents and his brothers Paddy, Christy, Joe, Seamus, Robert and sister Lizzie. Joe was a baker in Inglis bakery and he married a lovely girl from Keegan Street called Jean Douglas. Christy was a great motor mechanic. I never for the life of me see what there was about getting tucked into pig's feet, they were all gristle and fat but were always in great demand. To me the elder tasted like chicken and

Maggie would salt it and wrap it up in a sheet of paper. You can't get elder now days as it's tied up with offal and mad cows disease.

After getting tucked into the elder Spike Chuck and I would head round to Billy Edge's pub. You could slip in through the side door after hours and join in a sing song with Peter Campbell who would give us a rendition of the Dean Martin classics. Peter lived in Lagan Street beside the children's play ground and the hide and skin stores. His cousin Tommy Franklin lived with his mother Ginny in Campbell's Place and both Peter and Tommy worked as tailors making men's suits. They learned their trade while they were residents in the boy's home at Milltown, beside Milltown Cemetery, which was run by the Christian Brothers. They were put into care for playing truant from school. Some children ended up there for numerous reasons including stealing a bar of chocolate, a pack of cigs or vandalism to name but a few. I knew a few others from around the Markets who spent time in these institutions. These children, some as young as eight, were classed as criminals which they weren't but were treated as such. The judiciary and the Catholic hierarchy kept these boys institutions going with a steady influx of children from the working class districts of Belfast. The Catholic Church was paid by the state for each inmate they housed; the buildings were old and run down with rows of Victorian windows. A lot of these children were abused physically, mentally and sexually by some of the Christian Brothers who ran it and to have been incarcerated in this hell hole must have been a horrendous experience for these children. If any of these children are still living today they should be compensated big time and the Catholic Church and the judiciary should make apologies for any hurt and wrong that they caused. Surely this isn't such a big ask for robbing a child of his childhood.

Chapter 10

Working In The Bakery

Matt Dalton had a grocer's shop in Welsh Street and a fish and chip shop across the road in Stanfield Street and he was married to Mary McAllister, sister of John who was nicknamed Cheeky. John, what a character he also had two other sisters called Alice and Margaret who were lovely girls. They all worked in the shop and they were great workers and that also applied to his sons. His youngest and namesake Matt was a good footballer who played for Cromac Albion. Matt senior would mostly work in the fish and chip shop and his fish were something else, they would have melted in your mouth. Getting back to Cheeky John, he sometimes worked in the fruit market as a checker with his brother Neily. John liked to work with a pencil behind his ear, he was a good card player too and could read the cards like no one else. Cheeky was fond of a wee drink and a gamble and you wouldn't want to be his partner in cards and make a mistake as he would come down on you like a ton of bricks.

Cheeky John was standing in the bookies this day and was waiting on a horse to come in to get a double up. There was a fella standing beside him who had also backed the same horse and was cheering it on as it was well clear going to the last fence, on clearing the last it crashed on landing. John turned to him saying you would stop pigs and from that day on the guy got the nickname Pig Stopper. Sometimes we would work the evening shift at Inglis bakery which was from six in the evening till six the next morning and on the odd occasion you might have wanted to get off and go for a drink and it was on occasions such as these that when you're break came along you went looking for Cheeky John. For a small financial reward you would ask John could he ring up your department and make out that a certain family member usually a granny or granddad had passed away, even though for the most part in many an instance they had passed on many years before. You would give him the name of your foreman which in most instances was usually Vinci Hazzard and John would tell him your plight and he wouldn't take no for an answer. If Hazzard was turning him down he would put the sad voice on.

"How could you deny Big Dan on this sad occasion the chance to mourn the loss of a loved one with his close family and friends" he would say and that usually did the trick.

He was a class act alright, was Cheeky John, you would later meet him in Tommy Callen's bar and get him a few pints and you would always get a good laugh the way he told the story.

Inglis bakery was a large building facing our street, it stood five storey's high and ran the full length from Stuart Street down Eliza Street to Welsh Street. We baked everything from plain bread to cream buns and I worked in all departments at one stage or another. Rumour had it that Inglis's was run by the Orange Order. I was never tied to one flat as we called each department because there were no permanent jobs for the likes of me. We would stand at the front gate and if someone did not turn up for work you would be called in to replace them depending on who was first in line. You needed to be up early, about four in the morning to stand any chance of gaining a days employment as the early bird catches the worm so to speak. Some days I would go over around four and someone else would be there before me and it would usually be one of the Doherty's, Tommy, Willie or James who was nicknamed Bimbo.

"For fuck's sake did you stay up all night?" I would say laughing. I can recall us standing there in all kinds of weather rain, hail sleet or snow with biting freezing winds that turned any exposed skin red with the cold. All I can say is thank God for heavy jackets with deep pockets. The half six shift at the bakery was called the late shift as you did not finish till two thirty, if you started at five you finished at one o'clock. There were times when I was going to bed at eleven thirty and getting up at three thirty to head over to Inglis's front gate at four o'clock in the morning. Like I said we were there in hail rain or snow, it wasn't easy but you needed the work and most of all the money. The canteen opened at half six and if you did not get a start at least you could go up and get yourself a large fry with soda bread, potato bread, sausage and egg or as Bimbo called it the treatment. Sometimes we would sit there and play cards until the rest of the departments started work hoping to get a start ourselves and if Bimbo lost at the cards he would rip the deck up. He tore up so many decks that no one would ever lend us a deck to play with. I wonder why?

Wee Teeny Farmer was the cook in the Inglis canteen and she was fond of a gamble and would have a bet on the dogs at Dunmore and Celtic Park. She would look up the results the morning papers, if her bet was beat you would get burnt soda and sausage and the eggs were like rubber but if she won you would get a double fry up. Teeny also loved to play the one armed bandits and this particular day she was playing this machine in one of the bars around Cromac Square when she ran out of change. Teeny went up to the bar to get some ten pence pieces when Eddie Pinkie walked up to the machine, put in a ten pence piece and won the jackpot, a staggering twenty pounds. Of course Teeny demanded that Eddie give the winnings to her but there was no chance of that happening as Eddie Pinkie was still holding on to his confirmation money. Not long after I said to Pinkie jokingly.

"If I were you I would stay clear of the canteen as you know hell hath no fury like a woman scorned."

All joking aside though, wee Teeny Farmer was a real character with a heart of corn and she had three sons who also worked in the bakery, Michael, Jimmy and Charlie.

The flat next to the plain bread was where the soda farls, potato bread, pancakes and wheaten were baked by the ladies. It used to be called Jinkies. Hughie Nichole who wore the red collar was the foreman and big June Scott who wore the green collar was the charge hand, a lovely big girl I had my eye on from the word go. I was employed for a couple of weeks in this flat and it was handy enough as big June was giving the orders.

"Danny, would you go behind the oven. Danny, would you go on the escalator."

"Anything for you June" I would reply laughing.

I remember one day I began day dreaming about what it might be like if I were hitched to big June.

"I think I will go down to the bar June and get myself a few pints."

"Aye sure, after you mow the lawn and by the way the hall needs painting and papering and then you can do the dishes etc etc."

This was long before the dishwashers appeared on the scene. Horrors of horrors I thought to myself this is the stuff nightmares are made of because big June wasn't half demanding. Big June if you ever read this I'm just having a wee laugh.

The escalator was where you put the trays of sodas, potato bread, pancakes and wheaten which went down to the packing room on wooden trays. It would then be stacked in a trolley which back in the day was known as a boogie and you would have to go down to the ground floor to retrieve the empty ones and take them up on the lift. Now this lift went up to the top floor which was the flour loft, you would be ringing the bell for it to descend and you could be standing there for at least ten minutes waiting and wondering what floor it was on. I remember on one particular occasion when I had to run up the back stairs and check each floor to see who was using the lift. When I reached the flour loft I opened the exterior lift door and noticed that the interior door was open and the lights were out which meant the lift would not descend. That's when I realized that Bimbo Doherty must have been up to his old tricks again. I met him in the store room later on that day.

"For fuck sake Bimbo when are you going to grow up" I said laughing.

"Not guilty Big Dan" was Bimbo's reply.

That was Bimbo, a likeable rogue if ever there was one.

The last day in Jinkies was to be my lucky day. We would get our pay chit on a Friday, a couple of hours before we finished our shift, so on this particular day I went round to crying Al McMurray's bookies to place a bet on the horses. Al's was situated at the corner of Lagan Lane and I invested five shillings on a treble as I only earned one pound fifty for a day's wage. While I was in the bookies two of my results came in and I had two winners at odds of seven to two and four to one which meant I had about four pounds fifty going on to my last horse called Pink China, which was running in the next race. However I couldn't wait as I had to get back to work because I knew big June would be wondering what was keeping me so I hurried out of the crying Al's and on towards my work. When I got to the flat the foreman was doing my work on the escalator but the only thing I could think about was did my horse get up. I had been working away for at least twenty minutes when Con Eagan walked by.

"What won that race" I said to Con as I knew Con liked a punt himself.

"What did you call the winner" I said.

Con came over to where I was working, it was a horse called Pink China at thirty three to one. At that point I dropped a tray of sodas down the escalator as the bet paid out about one hundred and thirty pounds, which in today's currency would amount to about fifteen hundred quid or more.

In those days the bookies had a limit on all bets, robbing bastards that they were, so I only picked up fifty pounds but even so that was around six weeks wages back then. I had about two hours to go until my shift finished but I had no intention of spending the next two hours putting bread down an escalator especially when I had a few quid in my tail. I spotted Skinny Reynolds coming out of the plain bread section.

"Skinny" I shouted gesturing for him to come over to where I was working.

"Listen Skinny, I've only an hour left to go here so if you let me away early I'll give you a full day's pay" I said. I couldn't tell him how much I won because knowing Skinny he would have been looking for two days wages.

"Big Dan my shift is finished it's a Friday and I'm off for a gargle" and with that he bolted.

"Thanks a million Skinny" I shouted after him. I thought to myself I'm here till the death for fuck sake and that's when I spotted big June coming down the side of the oven. I called her over and looking her straight in the eye I said.

"June I can feel the flu coming on could you possibly get someone to cover for me so I can head on home and put my head down?"

Now big June was looking at me with those big dolly eyes of hers.

"Give me five minutes" she said and true to her word she returned with Susan Archer who was my mate Eddie Meehans wee cousin to enable me to go home. Now I might have fooled big June but definitely not Susan who called me over before I left.

"Don't be getting too drunk tonight Dan" she said smiling.

All the while June was insisting I get a hot lemon drink when I get home.

"It's the best thing to take for a flu" said June.

"Aye I will indeed June" I replied.

Women, what would you do without them, they love to fuss over you when you're ill. With that I slowly walked towards the stairs, turned round and waved back to big June. What an actor I was and of course when I was out of sight I took the stairs six at a time, bolted out the front gate and straight up to the bookies to collect my winnings.

I won about fifty pounds or ten big white fivers what ever way you want to look at it.

"How did you pick those winners" crying Al said as he was paying me out.

"What about all the losers I backed before that" I said.

"I'm only getting some of my money back after all."

I went straight round to the house and gave Aunt Kitty a few quid, got dressed, had something to eat and out for a few celebratory jars. The next morning Spike McCormack and I headed down to the train station to catch the Dublin train and three hours later we arrived at Dublin's Connolly station.

Chapter 11

The Honeymoon From Hell

We went looking for a bed and breakfast and the first door we rapped was answered by some old doll with her hair standing up on her head and a bottle of stout in her hand. She looked like a right nasty piece of work.

"What do you want?" she shouted.

"Do you think the woman next door would give us a drink of water?" says Spike and with that she slammed the door on our faces and I fell up against the wall laughing. So we went around a few more streets till we found the bed and breakfast where we would eventually stay. The landlady seemed friendly enough as she told us the rules of the house and she said to us.

"I hope you lads have a good memory for faces because the mirror in the bathroom is smashed.

After getting sorted we then headed down into the town for something to eat to fill our stomachs in preparation for a serious gargle. Mooney's Bar just off O'Connell Street was our first port of call. When we entered the bar the first thing I noticed were these large mirrors around the walls encased in carved mahogany wooden frames and the large marble counters and pillars and iron wrought tables. All their bars were fitted out with the same décor even the one situated in Belfast's Corn Market. They were cool in the summer and warm in the winter as they had these large fire places and the tiles on the floor and around the bar area must have cost a fortune. We ordered pork pies with brown sauce and washed them down with pints of porter. It has been stated that Mooney's served the best pint of Guinness in Ireland and I for one wouldn't doubt that for one minute. After a few pints we decided to go sightseeing around some of the finest drinking establishments in Dublin City.

The place was buzzing with people coming and going and the bars were jam packed. I strolled into the bookies to do a bet, I had two pound on one which came in at five to one and a pound each way on one that won giving me odds of seven to two and another bet which lost. Time to call it quits I thought to myself and my winnings for the day which was about fifteen pound would pay for the weekend, now days it wouldn't get you three pints. I walked outside to see where Spike was but there was no sign of him, he was well known for disappearing at times and then he would appear as if from nowhere. I had a brother in law who used to do the same thing, Gerry Davis, he would be drinking in your company and then all of a sudden he would disappear and then no matter where we moved to Gerry would suddenly show up again as if by magic.

"Where did you get to" I would say to him.

"I met an old friend in the bookies and we had a few pints together" he would say.

Sure you could never fall out with Gerry as he had this personality about him that gave anyone who ever met him the feel good factor. Gerry was to die of lung cancer in his late thirties and he never smoked a cigarette in his life, always the way.

After leaving the bookies I dandered about O'Connell Street stopping off at a few watering holes along the way. However it wasn't long until I began to feel the effects of the Guinness kicking in so I called into a wee chipie and treated myself to a fish supper. I then found myself a bench, sat down and ate and when I had finished I just lay back and took in the sights. One of the first things to catch my eye was Nelson's Column. The British sea lord, it stood about one hundred and thirty four feet, a bastion of British rule that was yesteryear, looking down over the Irish peasants below and signifying that they once ruled the roost here. It was a blot on the landscape to the Irish nation as a whole until it was so badly damaged in an explosion carried out by the Irish Republican Army in nineteen sixty six that it had to be totally removed. The planned demolition of the monument by Irish Army engineers caused more damage to the properties in and around O,Connell Street than did the original IRA attack. Maybe they should have turned a blind eye like Nelson and let the IRA finish the job as it must have cost them a bomb [pardon the pun] to repair all the damage that was caused. A few years after the event someone wrote a song about it, as is the Irish way, they will write a song about nearly anything. It was called Up Went Nelson In Old Dublin and if I am to be frank here I must admit that it must be one of the worst songs I have ever heard in my life. Although the fact is that the only ones who missed Nelson's Pillar in Dublin were the pigeons and the sea gulls who now needed to find another high point to perch on and shit on the general population below.

It was a beautiful warm sunny Saturday afternoon even though it was October and still there was no sign of Spike. When you think about it now days you could just lift you're mobile phone but back in the day we were still at the smoke and mirror signal stage. I sat smoking and watching the ladies stroll by and they were something else I must say mostly dark haired colleens making their way into town to shop presumably. I began to recall my antics in the dance halls back in Belfast. I would be dancing with some girl thinking what to say.

"Do you come here often" I would blurt out, or "Do you think it is going to rain outside."

Then noticing the bored look on her face wishing this dance would just end so she could get away. I made myself out to be a total edjit because I was still too shy when it came to the fairer sex. Fuck this I thought to myself I am off to get a gargle and I immediately headed for the nearest pub which was across the street. You could here the music from outside and as I opened the door and stepped inside nobody took any notice and why should they as everyone seemed to be having a great time.

There was a four man group in the corner of the bar churning out a variety of country and western songs. I joined in with some company and we continued to drink and sing all through the night. After about ten pints of Guinness and half a dozen whiskeys the old demon drink was taking its toll and judging by the amount I had consumed I would like to think so. It was getting dark outside as I looked at my watch and realized that it was one o'clock in the morning and it was time I should be getting back to my digs. I couldn't think straight and come to that I couldn't walk straight either so I decided to ask the bar man to call me a taxi and he pointed to my feet.

"There's your taxi" he said laughing.

As it was closing time and the bar man did indeed get me a taxi which I jumped into, well maybe I wasn't so energetic, so one could say I fell in. I gave the cab driver the address of my digs which was about ten minutes drive away and we eventually arrived about half an hour later.

"How much do I owe you" I asked the driver,

"That will be three pounds" he replied.

"I was only looking a lift to my digs mate, I don't want to buy your taxi mucker" I said

"Well if you don't want to pay I can always call the guards" he said.

All of a sudden the danger signs were flashing through my intoxicated brain. Cops, prison, a cell, a kicking with steel toe capped boots, court, a big fine or worse still jail time. I could picture myself getting banged up for three months, what a nightmare scenario. I put my head to his car window.

"How much did you say I owed you" I asked.

"Three pounds" he replied.

"Why didn't you say that in the first place" I said and threw the money at him, at which he gave me the fingers.

"Fuck you" I shouted and he sped off. The guards don't take kindly to anyone from the black north as they called it coming down to the south and giving the locals a hard time.

I opened the door of the digs and slipped into the house. It was in darkness and not a sound could be heard and I crept up the stairs being careful not to waken anyone. I opened my bedroom door easily and wasn't sure if it was my head or the room that was spinning. I didn't bother to undress as I couldn't because I was too drunk. So I stretched out my arms like Our Lord on the cross and fell back on top of the bed and at that moment a woman jumped up on the bed and let out an unmerciful scream and I'm almost certain her husband did also. The landlady ran in and grabbed me by the arm and led me out of the room.

"I was trying to get in touch with you all day" she said

"I moved you both into another room and put a honeymoon couple into your room."

When she led me to our new room I hit the sack like nobody's business.

Waking up early the next morning I nearly fell over Spike, who at this point, was lying beside his bed sprawled out on the floor fully clothed and fast asleep. I went into the bathroom, had a shower, got dressed and headed out to get some breakfast as I didn't want to bump into the honeymoon couple as it would have been too embarrassing. I felt like someone had hit me on the head with a hammer, a massive hangover or what? I found a wee café and ordered a mug of hot tea and a fry. After getting stuck into and finishing my breakfast I stepped outside and lit up a cigarette. It was a warm sunny morning and there people going about the place, some on their way to church and others heading to the shop for the Sunday papers but unfortunately fortunately for me bars would not open till mid day and it was only nine thirty in the morning. Jesus Christ I thought to myself it would be another two and a half hours till I could get the hair of the dog. I went to the nearest phone box and dialled the landlady's digs to see if Spike was awake yet.

"I think he is, hold on a second and I'll tell him you're on the phone" she said.

Spike came on the phone.

"Did you go to mass" he asked.

I cried with laughter.

"Me going to chapel, are you having me on Spike? I'm sitting in a café here nursing my hangover. How could I sit in some chapel and sit for an hour listening to some oul lad talking a load of fucking rubbish. Listen, meet me here in half an hour" I said mentioning the name and address of the café.

"Right you got it" replied Spike.

I headed back into the café and ordered an ice cold milkshake then, a bowl of chicken soup, then another milkshake but no matter what I took the hangover wouldn't leave me. I only had two options here I thought, either I could go off the drink, lead a clean and wonderful life and never feel sick the next morning or I could enjoy a gargle, live life to the full and to hell with the self inflicted wounds.

Unfortunately I choose the latter. I had just finished yet another milkshake when Spike ambled through the door, Jesus he looked rough.

"Do you want a fry" I asked him.

"No, the landlady made me beans and toast" he mumbled.

I can recall Our Hanna telling me a joke a few years earlier about something similar. This fellow landed a job in Dublin and when he booked into this bed and breakfast the landlady asked him what he would like for breakfast.

"Beans and toast and give me loads of beans" he said.

The next morning he received his breakfast and went on to his work. A few hours later a Garda raps her door and informs her that they had fished a man out of the river and that he had a suicide note on him with the landlady's address on it.

"Yes he booked in here yesterday" said the landlady.

"When he left here this morning did he look alright to you? Asked the officer.

"Oh God yes, when he left here he was full of beans" said the landlady.

Spike was too sick to laugh but when I told him about the honeymoon couple he was doubled over laughing.

"I swear to fuck Spike, I was full drunk and I am almost sure her husband also jumped up and screamed" said I.

This called for another round of laughter and all that day I would think about it and burst out laughing.

"Spike" says I. "I know we are meant to stay another night but after that episode I'm going back home today but for now why don't we dander up to the nearest bar till I get a cure."

"I'm all for that" says Spike.

We needn't hurry ourselves as it was still half an hour till opening time.

"By the way where the fuck did you get too last night" I said.

"I honesty can't remember big Dan. I had no idea where I went till I woke up on the floor this morning."

We entered the first bar we came to and what a pokey wee hole it was too, you couldn't have swung a cat in it. There were already some punters standing at the bar and as we walked up to it a couple of them turned round to see who we were. I ordered a couple of pints of Guinness and they must have heard my Northern accent.

"Are you down on holiday? One of them asked.

"Aye" said I.

"When are you going back home?" He asked.

"Today" I answered.

Jesus Christ I thought talk about some fucking nosey people. Spike and I lifted our pints and moved over to an empty table and pulled out a couple of seats. After four pints or so I was feeling a lot better, so would anyone for that matter. We looked up the times of the trains to Belfast and seen that there was one departing at three thirty.

"That'll do us Spike" said I.

"I couldn't be bothered going back to the digs for all we have there" said Spike.

"I'll buy you another razor" I answered and with that we left our gear in the digs, made our way up to the train station and boarded the three thirty to Belfast, home to dear old Aunt Kitty.

When we arrived at Great Victoria Street station, where the Europa hotel is now, we were approached by this man, tall, thin, going grey and wearing a long rain coat, I immediately thought flasher and looked behind me surely there had to be a woman in the vicinity and he wasn't about to flash Spike and I.

"Would you both mind stepping into this office" he said and pointed the way.

Spike asked him who he was.

"RUC" he replied.

"What is it you want" I asked.

"You were both observed going into phone booths in Dublin and using the phone, who were you phoning?" He asked.

"Dan Breen" Spike shouted in his face and the guy turned white as a sheet. I could see his hand trembling and I jumped in to defuse the situation.

"We were phoning our landlady to see what time she closed up for the night as we might be late" I answered.

There was a long stoney silence and he kept staring at us for what seemed like an eternity.

"Ok lads you can go now" he said.

With that we turned, walked out of the office and straight down to the Market. I later found out that he was a Special Branch man, he never asked for our names, which might seem strange but I guess he knew them already. On the way home I said to Spike.

"Who the fuck'is Dan Breen?"

We were never really taught any Irish history at school and I never would have known then who he was.

"I used to hear my Da talking about him. He fought down south during the war of independence in the twenties." said Spike.

"Well he didn't do much for us up here when they can follow us all round Dublin and back up to Belfast, watching our every move" I said. As we got to the markets it was about nine o clock and time to retire for the night I thought. We got to Staunton Street and I said my goodbyes to Spike as he turned into Campbell's Place. As I walked into the house and put my head around the door, Aunt Kitty was sitting on the settee having her tea.

"Did you miss me" I said to Aunt Kitty.

"Sure you were only away for two days and I was not expecting you home till tomorrow" she said.

"But I got homesick and there's no place like home as you always say Aunt Kitty." I was only keeping her going.

"Do you want anything to eat son?" She said.

"No I'm ok I got something earlier on and I'm going to retire early as I have to get up for work."

Chapter 12

The Railroad Squad

Next morning I struggled out of bed and looked at the clock, it was four am so I needed to stick my kite under the water tap which was freezing. I got dressed and headed over to Inglis bakery which was just across the road from our house and I put my name in the book and low and behold I was actually first in line for a change. I lit up a cigarette while I was waiting for the canteen to open which wouldn't be till at least five thirty. Then the Doherty's arrived Bimbo, Tommy and Willie. I told them about our escapades in Dublin and the three of them burst out laughing. Willie, who suffered from asthma, went into a fit of coughing and couldn't catch his breath so had to retire to the house for medication. It was now five thirty and the canteen was opening up so I informed Joe Butler who was the time keeper where we were going and asked him to give us a shout if there was any work going. I bought the fry's and we were almost finished eating when Joe Butler came on the intercom.

"Will Danny Mulcahy, James and Tommy Doherty please report to the plain bread."

I headed up to the locker room, put on my white overalls and within minutes I was standing at the back of the oven waiting for the plain bread to emerge a ticket at a time, a ticket being four loaves of batch bread.

I would then place the bread on wooden trays and place the trays in a trolley or boogie as we called them and transported them down to the cooler where most were sliced and the rest sold as they were. As I was emptying the oven on my own because my helper was down in the score room (so named because we received twenty minutes for our break hence the score room) as we called it having a smoke, I spotted Norman Wetherall. He was putting the pan bread on to trays as it came up from what we called the iron lung oven and just like myself, he then put it on trays and boogies in order to transport it to the cooler room for slicing. Suddenly I noticed an altercation breaking out and Wetherall seemed to be restraining this fellow who was in between himself and Cecil Holiday the foreman. Norman took a hammer from the guys hand as it was coming down on the foreman's head. As it turned out the hammer wielding guy had been covering in the same job for the past four months for the regular guy who was out on the sick. Vincie Hazzard a green collar man had misinformed the guy that it was Cecil Holiday the red collar foreman that made out the rota and that in his [Hazzard's] opinion that if you were first in you would be last out. However that wasn't the case, if you were working in a regular mans job, you would stay in that position until such time as the regular guy came back and then you would be at the back of the queue again. Weatherall was telling me later on that had he not intervened, that he firmly believed the guy would have killed the foreman. Weatherall would later make a joke about this incident as he did about everything else. He never took life serious and had to be one of the funniest characters I have ever met. He was married to a lovely wee girl called Marie Murray and they made a lovely couple. After all the commotion I was due my break and I headed straight for the canteen. As I was going down the stairs I bumped into big June with them big dolly eyes, Jesus they would have melted any mans heart.

"Well did you get over your flu" she said.

"Just about June I feel a lot better now" said I trying to keep a straight face as I hid my blushes.

The weekend hangover was beginning to lift now so feeling better I asked.

"Do you want to go for a cup of tea" trying to change the subject from my flu.

"I can't, I have to get back to work" she said rushing on by.

"I'll see you later June" said I and headed for the canteen.

When I returned I went on the dough cutting machine, so I could let young John Maththews away for his break, he was plating the plain bread on to the oven and I could work both jobs.

"I'll only be half an hour, I'm only going round to my granny's who just lives in Annette Street" he says.

An hour and a half had passed when in strolls the bold John who was all smiles.

"Did you get the last train home from Cork? I didn't know your granny had moved down south" Then I added.

"Right Big John I'm finished time to go home."

"You can't do that" he said.

 "Who can't just watch me" I said laughing.

I passed by what we used to call the Bisto's department and how it got it's name was because there was an old foreman who was previously based in the department who looked like one of the Bisto kids in the advertisement. In this department they baked the Vienna rolls, baps and the small brown hovis loaf. We jobbers tried to give this place a wide berth as you had to start at eight o'clock in the morning and work until half four in the afternoon, which in my mind was far too late in the day, especially since you have been up from four that morning. It definitely wasn't for me, fuck that I thought to myself that's like a twelve hour shift.

Wee Walter Ligget was now the foreman in the Bisto department and was in the baking end before being promoted. I remember back when I was about sixteen years old and there was Eddie Meehan and I walking up the Ormeau Road. It was the twelfth of July and a beautiful sunny day and we had just reached the Ballynafeigh orange hall facing the Curzon picture house. The band were playing God save the queen with their banners and flags lowered and we just walked on by thinking nothing of it. Then all of a sudden they made a charge at us with their pikes and swords and pinned us against the wall of the orange hall. I mean now when you think about it , these were big men harassing children. Just at that moment a voice in the background shouted out.

"Leave them kids alone I know them" and it was Wee Walter Ligget who was part of the parade. He ran over and got in between the orange mob and us and then they backed off and Walter made sure we were safely out of harms way. Eddie Meehan had been serving his time as an apprentice baker at Inglis's at the time and Walter must have recognized him from work. Just as well for us or God knows what would have happened. I'll never forget what Wee Walter did for us and he was a true gentleman in my eyes.

Then you had the pastry department. In my opinion this department was wee buns to work in [pardon the pun]. David DD Conlon, chucks brother worked there and he was tasked with carrying out a number of chores to complete during the course of his shift. One of his chores was to empty the fly catcher trays, you know the type with the blue lighting and electric bars to kill the flies. We would often wind him up about putting the dead flies into the currant square mix. He took it all in good steam. Now don't let my comment about the flies in the currant square mix put you off them, for when they're baked you can't tell the difference and they actually make a nicer flavour, only keeping you going here. I worked in this department a few times over the years and I used to bring the meat pies home to Aunt Kitty, as these pies were made with the best of mince steak. She never had to buy sodas, pancakes or potato bread. I also worked the night shift on occasion and that's when they made the coconut fingers, snow balls and jam doughnuts. I would inject the jam into the doughnuts and would make sure and fill them to the brim during my shift. I must say when I was in charge of the jam, the sales of the doughnuts would go through the roof.

On the ground floor you had Charlie Graffs where they baked the barn braks, milk scones and fruit loaves. We would always try and give this department a wide berth as you would be required to work until five pm. Spike and I eventually got ourselves permanent jobs in the yard squad. They were trying to do away with the jobbers which meant that if there was a man short in any of the departments then one of the yard squad would step in to replace him. On numerous occasions there were so many men out, that the jobber's services were still required. Our job was to keep the yard clear of trollies or boogies as they were called and transport them on the lift to the various departments. One morning we heard Joe Butler the time keeper calling our names over the intercom saying that we were to report to Charlie Graffs. Then the panic stations set in, so we headed to the flour loft and freedom. Joe Butler was still calling us every five minutes and this went on for about half an hour before silence ensued.

"Don't rush" I said to Spike. "We will descend in about ten minutes."

Spike suggested we splash flour around our boots and whites, then, we could make out that there was a flour spill and we were clearing it up.

"Good thinking" I said.

We later found out that Pat McCarthy a neighbour of ours who lived facing Spike in Campbell's Place, was railroaded into the job and to make things worse the man whose job Pat was assigned was going to be out for approximately four months, unfortunately for Pat. The yard foreman asked us where we had disappeared to and we told him about the fictional flour spillage that we needed to clean up.

"Have a look at my boots and overalls" I said. "Do you think we are telling you lies" and with that he walked off. Spike and I walked past Pat who was working behind the oven and the sweat was lashing out of him. He shouted over to us.

"Two fly men you are"

"Will you keep me two of those barn braks for my tea Pat? I shouted back.

"Fuck off Big Dan" came the reply.

Pat took the following week off thinking when he came back that someone else would be in the job possibly Spike or me but it was not to be, for we had railroaded Jimmy Marlow the union shop steward into the job so when Pat returned he was sent straight back to his new post. I don't know how Pat did it but he later got moved to the pastry department. A wee man called Mo McGivern who lived in Sally the ducks house in Stanfield Street ended up getting landed with the job. After that we were nicknamed the rail road squad. Pat McCarthy later joined the SDLP and would later be a future lord mayor and if you're reading this Pat, I'd love to know how on earth you managed to wrangle your transfer to the pastry department.

Chapter 13

Geordie Stow Is As Fly As They Go

Peter Valentine, the yard foreman in Inglis bakery asked Spike and I to get rid of all the old scrap that was lying around the yard, such as lids, Pipes, old boogies and the like, looking at it I guessed it to be around a ton in weight.

"And get rid of that old safe that's lying over there in the corner" said Valentine.

My eyes lit up at the mention of the safe as that old thing must have weighed at least another ton. The safe was about seven feet tall with two large doors.

"I'll go round to Stow's yard and see if we can get rid of all this scrap iron" I said to Spike.

Just as I was walking down Welsh Street, who should be coming up towards me but the bold Geezer, the very man I was looking for

"Come and have a look at this scrap and tell me what you think" said I as we walked into the yard which was situated in McCauley Street, this was where the Inglis flour silo stood. In later years Geordie Stow was to acquire this property when Inglis bakery closed down and extended his scrap business which he had built up from his own house in Eliza Street just beside St Coleman's school. He got demobbed from the army and he came over from England and got married to a local girl called Cathleen whom he had met while he was stationed here during the war.

Geordie would work till the wee small hours every night braking up old army lorries with just a sledge hammer and brute force. Stack McCartan and Gypsie Lavelle would also bring Geordie up to Long Kesh which was a disused airfield at the time and where they would dismantle scrap airplanes. Years later Geordie would become a millionaire and believe me he earned every penny of it with his bare hands.

Back at the yard Geezer took a look at the scrap and then spotted the safe and took a close look at the name on the safe. It was a Chubb safe.

"I'll go round and see Stow" he said and with that he hurried off.

Ten minutes or so had passed and lo and behold coming in through the gates were Geordie and his crew, Buster Brown, Young Tony, Patsey Magee, a fork lift truck and a flat bed lorry. We should have clicked on then but we did not. Stow took a look at the scrap and shook his head

"Pewter metal" he said in his English accent.

"Not worth shit" and he still hasn't looked at the safe.

"I'll give you forty pounds for the whole lot" said Stow.

I looked over at Spike who then nodded his approval

"Ok Geordie you've got yourself a deal" and with that he instructed his men to begin loading the lorry.

When all the scrap had been lifted I thought he was forgetting about the safe but not a chance of it Stow then told his men to take the old safe and with that Buster Brown jumped on a fork lift and carried the safe out through the front gate. We got forty pounds for the lot.

"Ah well it didn't cost us anything" I said to Spike.

We gave the foreman a fiver and split the rest. We later heard that the safe was top of the range and that Geordie put it in the auctions, where it fetched around seven hundred pounds which was a tidy sum in those days. Well, what did we know about safes anyhow? You live and learn the hard way I suppose. I didn't blame Geezer either because he wouldn't have gotten much of Stow anyhow but I bought him twenty fags anyway.

Further up Eliza Street lived the Pinkies, Eugene the father and his sons Eddie,Charlie, and Tommy. They all worked at Inglis bakery and the father Eugene worked in the flour silo. He was also into eletronics and radios and he ended up building his own television set before anyone else in the Markets ever possessed one. Then there was the McCabes Jim and Annie, who's maiden name was Lagan. Annie's brother Eddie who I still see on a regular basis now lives in the New Lodge and who could forget her other brother Billy, better known as Buckie who was a real character and her eldest brother Jimmy Lagan, they were a good family. Jim McCabe worked as an electrician in the giant crane in the shipyard which we used to call Tom Thumb and his son also named Jim worked alongside him and the McCabes also had a daughter called Alice.

A couple of doors up you had the McGarry's and the last house was the Wigblit's, the father was an English man. I used to mate about with his son who we called Eddie Wigwam. We would hang out at the top of Eliza Street and Stewart Street with Alex McChristen and Tom Fitzsimmons. The Dobbins lived in the first house in Stewart Street, big Seamus and Charlie and their sister Patsey and they all worked in the bakery. Fast forward a couple of years when the troubles broke out and Charlie Dobbin was telling me that he was walking up the Falls Road to see what was happening. Greaves's mill was blazing and the place was in turmoil, when he got to the corner of Clonard Street and there was groups of men standing at the street corners. Then out of the blue this crowd of men ran past him. There must be another riot he thought to himself. They ran into the pub and it was only then that he realized what was happening. They were running from the bookies to the bar to see a race on the television while the place was burning down around them, nothing was going to stop them from having a wee flutter.

Chapter 14

From Freedom To Slavery (Marriage)

The fifties brought out the Teddy boy style with the long coats and drain pipe trousers and the spongy sole shoes. Some guys had these long grey coats with fur on the collars, pockets and cuffs with lace string ties. Davy Crawford from the Short Strand and Big Mokie Roberts from New Bond Street were the first to were this particular style as for myself, I preferred to stick to the plain dark navy coat. Most of us would go around to Burton's and get them tailor made, now days they just stick a block of plastic in one end of a machine and a suit comes out the other, no need for tailors here. The dance halls in the fifties and early sixties were booming, every night there was some dance hall in full swing and rocknroll was the new sound. Bill Haley and the Comets, Elvis, Roy Orbinson, Gerry Lee Lewis, Buddy Holly, Tom Jones, Willie Nelson and Gerry and the Pacemakers to name but a few. I am a country and western fan myself, Johnny Cash, Tommy Wynette, Hank Williams and Slim Whitman were among my favourites. Oh to be able to sing and yodel like Slim Whitman, it would have required a very painful operation and marriage would have been out of the question.

The Plaza was in Chichester Street and it would open on Wednesday afternoon which was a half day for the shop working staff and also a Friday and Saturday night. What you need to remember is that there was no alcohol consumption permitted on the premises and that applied to all the dance halls and if you looked under the weather, half cut or pissed, you would be refused entry. The Fiesta in Hamilton Street just of Cromac Street was one of the many dance halls that we frequented during those golden years. There was the Jig in Coaches Street just off Townsend Street on the Falls Road, John Dossers in High Street, Clarks Royal Avenue was great and when Sunday night came about it would be either the Dall in Divis Street, the Orpheus York Street or the Kingsway in Castle Street where I met my future wife Patricia but that's another story. There were some great dancers around in those days but I most certainly wasn't one of them as I had two left feet or was it three? I remember this one night in the Plaza, when the dancing had just finished and we were on our way out the door, when someone ran in and shouted that the Canadian sailors were waiting outside to give us a tanking. This guy said there were about a couple of hundred of them. The previous week a couple of Canadian war ships sailed into Belfast Harbour and since then there had been ongoing fights between the sailors and the locals. In particular there was this big Canadian sailor who stood around seven feet tall and about six feet broad he reminded me of Bluto out of the Popeye show. The Plaza foyer was crowded by now and no one would make the move to venture outside. I was going to but was held back. It's as we'll I'm writing this isn't it? A suggestion was made to send someone round to the Markets to get Silver McKee but I fear Bluto would have picked Silver up and put him in his back pocket as the auld saying goes. We looked outside and could see the sailors were still there and Big Bluto was punching the walls at this point. I thought I could feel the building shaking as he was gathering up steam. Eventually the Plaza doormen called the cops and that's how we were eventually able to get out. Everyone made a bolt for the doors and freedom.

One Friday night Eddie Meehan and I after a few pints in Gil Maguires in Cromac Street decided to head off to the Kingsway dance hall off Castle Street. He was to meet his girlfriend Patsy McCormack who hailed from Carrick Hill and her three mates, Duchess Parker, Susie Clark and Patsy Davis. After we were introduced my eyes immediately lit on Patsy Davis, she was tall, slim and pretty with long blond hair. Now here was me who was used to eying up the dark haired women for most of my adult life now finding myself attracted by a blond right away. I asked her for a dance and then proceeded to take her around the floor. Rock n roll music was just coming out then and I must admit Patricia was a good dancer but it's a pity I couldn't say the same about myself. I had two left feet and they seemed to be sharing the same shoe. Most of the dance halls in them days had their own bands as the DJs came on the scene a number of years later. We danced for most of the night until it was time to go and I then walked her home to Upper Library Street in the Carrick Hill area and we planned to meet again the following week at the same venue, the Kingsway dance hall. Patsy and I continued to see each other and some weeks we take in a film at the cinema and on the weekends would treat ourselves to a drink or two in Conway's upstairs lounge in Fountain Street. A pint back then would have set you back around two shillings, a far cry from the almost four pounds or so it would cost you to purchase a similar product in some of the bars around the town now days. As time went by my nights out with the boys became less and less frequent and I was spending more and more time with Patsy. I think my roving days were finally coming to an end.

I was twenty years of age at the time and Patsy was a year younger than me at nineteen. Patsy worked at Barbour's spinning mill on the Shore Road. As patsy always worked a half day on Wednesday we would plan to meet up at the Plaza dance hall which catered for all the shop assistants who for the most part only worked a half day on Wednesdays. We would meet up with some of Patsy's mates who also worked in the mill and had the half day off. The dance would always finish at five in the afternoon on a Wednesday with Patsy and I agreeing to meet up again at the weekend. Aunt Kitty became ill around this time and she was taken into hospital. She was suffering from an iron deficiency which was causing a lot of problems with her health and she remained in the hospital for a couple of weeks. When Aunt Kitty was finally discharged from hospital she went to live with our Hanna until she regained her strength. I was working away in the bakery at the time and was working overtime when possible on the three to eleven shift. I would usually team up with big Gerry Hanna at the back of the oven striping the plain bread. Big Gerry's nickname was The Cat, he was good craic and not a week went by when he wouldn't have said.

"I'm finished with them horses Big Dan. Why should I give my hard earned money to some stranger I don't even know" and then the following week it would be the drink and I would burst out laughing.

"Gerry you are your own worst enemy. It's in your blood just like myself" I would say.

"Then I'll get a fucking blood transfusion" said Gerry laughing.

"It's a fucking head transplant you need Gerry" I quirked up.

"I'll go and get my break" he said before disappearing down the back stairs and I ran over and shouted after him.

"Don't be all fucking night now Gerry and remember I have to get my break also."

It was handy enough emptying the oven on my own, putting the bread onto a wooden tray before lifting it onto the escalator and the fact that I possessed a long reach helped me with the process.

I could also pull the bread back and take a ten minute break but you weren't really supposed to as you had to let the bread bake it's full time.

Patsy and I were now going out with each other for around a year when we eventually decided that we would be wed the following year. First of all it takes money to get married so money for gambling and drinking were out of the question. I wasn't even married yet but I still found it hard enough just getting the money up to do so. Unlike us fellas women are moulded for this marriage thing from they are knee high. They get the pram, the doll and the dolls house, early training for the tough years ahead. Women had to learn how to cook, clean, do the ironing and the household chores including the shopping. Not forgetting the most important task of childbearing. Boys wouldn't be asked to do any of these tasks as they were expected to be the breadwinners and follow their fathers into the bars and the bookies. Things are changing now days though, I see young men going shopping, child minding and pushing prams now albeit with their arms fully outstretched putting as much distance between themselves and the pram as possible. The man's world scenario seems to be coming to an end. I remember an old advert whereby this man is standing outside the supermarket and looking through the window he is seen miming to his wife asking her not to forget the Flora. Now days it's the other way round where he is in doing the shopping and she is standing on the outside with a fag in one hand and a vodka and coke in the other miming to him through the window don't forget the babies nappies, how times have changed.

So we planned to get married on December the twenty seventh, the day after Boxing day nineteen sixty in St Patrick' Church in Donegal St. Now who in their right mind gets married the day after Boxing Day? I was asked many a time after that. At least it is one date that I'll never forget I would say. Tragically in the October before, Patsy's younger brother Henry was knocked down and killed by a lorry on a pedestrian crossing, he was ten years old at the time. Naturally the family were distraught and it was very hard for all of them to deal with and the wedding plans came to a halt as you would expect. I went up to the wake and paid my respects to Patsy's mother and father Michael and Maggie Davis. It was a terrible time for the whole family and they never really got over it.

After a couple of months it was decided that the wedding would go ahead. The morning of the wedding Patsy's eldest brother Michael came down to the Markets to pick me up in the limo. Unfortunately Michael would also lose his life in tragic circumstances when he was involved in a car accident. Michael was doing the best man and Aunt Kitty was at the door as I was going out and I gave her a big hug and noticed that she had tears in her eyes. A few of the neighbours were standing around and they wished me all the best as I stepped into the car and headed off to the chapel. I can remember saying to myself this is it Big Dan no turning back now as I looked around the markets wondering, will it ever be the same again, no it fucking wont. I think there may have been a tear in my eye also, come on Big Dan pull yourself together I thought to myself. Anybody would think you were on your way to get executed and in some respects it certainly seemed that way. After all it was a big step for any young man and a giant leap for mankind, where do you think you are going, the fucking moon. Anyway we landed at the gates of Stalingrad, I mean the chapel, sorry Patsy I'm getting carried away here only joking.

We made our way to our intended seats and I sat beside Aunt Kitty. Just behind us were our Hanna and her husband Mickey Ferrin, my mother and step dad Charlie Treble, Aunt Alice and her husband Johnny Donaghy and aunt Cathleen with Joe Hinds. After about fifteen minutes Patsy and her father came walking down the aisle and what a sight to behold was Patsy. She was a vision in white with her blond hair, long dress and veil. Hope I've got this right, now that I'm looking back. Women dream all their lives for this moment, from the wee doll and pram to the big wedding day. So the time had come and the priest called us over to the Alter where we stood hand in hand. As previously stated Patsy's brother Michael was the best man and her cousin Martha Lavery was the bridesmaid. Martha's husband Peter was boxing at the time if I can remember correctly. Then it was time for all the formalities, do you take this woman, do you take this man, then the signing of the book, this was your contract, for better or for worse, in sickness and in health, for richer and for poorer and in the case of working class families it would usually be for poorer. When all was done and dusted we were Mr and Mrs Mulcahy, easy or not, so, easy, depending on how you look at it.

The reception was held at the Park Avenue Hotel over in East Belfast. Back in the fifties a lot of working class people would, for the most part hold the reception in their own homes as it was a hell of a lot less expensive and it was usually a breakfast. So we pushed the boat out and got ourselves a venue and at the Park Avenue Hotel. After the speeches and the meals we all settled down to listen to the music. I had a drink with Charlie Treble and my uncle Joe Hinds. Aunt Kitty had a couple of red wines which made her cry at the thought of my leaving home. I threw my arms around her in an effort to console her.

"Don't you worry Aunt Kitty, I'll be down every day and it will be as if I've never left home" I said but looking back on it I don't think she was totally convinced. As the day wore on I had a dance with our Hanna and my mother then Patsy and I went up to the hotel bedroom to get ready, for we were heading down to Dublin for our honeymoon. Off course now days it's the Caribbean or Spain.

We said our goodbyes and headed for the train station and a few hours later we landed in Dublin and went to a bed and breakfast that we had pre booked. After getting our room we got a shower and headed out into the city (well what else did you expect). Anyway Patsy did some shopping then we had a drink and a meal and as it was starting to get dark outside we decided we would head back to the digs. We were tired seeing as we had been awake from early that morning and before we retired for the night I placed a chair against the door to secure it.

"What's that for?" Patsy inquired.

"Just for precautionary measures dear, you never know, you might have some head case coming in the middle of the night mistaken our room for his" said I, as I never did tell her about my escapades the last time I was in Dublin.

Chapter 15

Our Family Begins

When we returned from our honeymoon we moved to patsy's old house in Upper Library St as her mother had moved to a house in Ellington St. After a few months Patsy was expecting our first child. I was over the moon but I knew that I would need to work a lot harder now and avail of all the overtime I could get my hands on. I also had to awaken a little earlier each morning as I was now required to walk from Carrick Hill down to Eliza St every morning but I was young and fit at the time so it wasn't any bother. Patsy and I decided that if the baby were to be a boy that we would name him Henry after both her brother and my father. Patsy gave birth to our child at her mother's house in Ellington St, just off the Old Lodge

Road. I was in the working kitchen having my tea when I received the news that the child was a boy. I can remember being overjoyed at the time but it was to be short lived as the midwife spotted something wrong and sent for the doctor who confirmed our worst fears. Our little boy had been born with Spina Bifida. It meant that he had a spinal defect in which the fluid that travels up and down the spine was being impeded resulting in a swelling of the brain among other complications. Henry lived until he was nine months old and if he were alive today he would be fifty three years old.

Apparently when Patsy was pregnant she had been taking some tablets that were supposed to ease the effects of morning sickness called Thalidomide, this drug was manufactured by a German drug company. It was withdrawn from the market after a very high percentage of the children of the many women who took it during pregnancy for morning sickness were noticed to be born with very serious birth defects. A few years after Henry was born a large number of children from all over the globe were born with very serious birth defects. It was horrible to witness those poor unfortunate children being born with such defects and to eventually discover that these defects were caused as a direct result of their mothers having ingested this drug which unbeknown to them would cause such horrific consequences. A guy who lived a few doors up from our house called David Loughern was born with no arms due to the effects of this drug and he died not so long ago at the age of forty five. I firmly believe that this drug company were responsible for the death of my first born child but it would have been near impossible to prove, especially back in the day. As you can imagine we were utterly devastated by the news of our little Henry. The doctor was talking away to me saying things like you'll have other children but that was too far into the future to even contemplate, all I could think about was our little Henry. Our son had probably just a few months to live, so every morning when we awoke, we would check to see if the swelling on his brain had increased. One morning Patsy couldn't get any response from Henry, so we rang the doctor who came out and pronounced him dead, it was just six months after his christening. We buried our son along with Patsy's grandparents in a burial plot located in Our Lady's Acre. I'll never forget that journey up to the graveyard with his small blue coffin on my knee. My mind was racing with these thoughts about having more children and hoping that we would be blessed with some more.

The following month was December and Aunt Kitty took ill and had to go into hospital. It was confirmed that she had developed cancer of the bowel and that it was in the early stages. Our Hanna, who was expecting at the time, accompanied me up to visit Aunt Kitty in the Mourne Hospital on the Whitewell Road. Aunt Kitty was in good spirits and she was expecting to be released soon. Our Hanna went and spoke to the doctor who at that point confirmed our worst fears. It was aggressive and she only had a few months left to live. In those days you were not informed if you were diagnosed with cancer, or how long you had to live, just next of kin and close family members were informed because I assume they thought it would be better for the patient. Aunt Kitty came home at Christmas to spend time with her family and she went up to stay with our Hanna in Andytown and we all had our Christmas dinner together. It proved to be her last Christmas as she passed away on the sixth of July nineteen sixty two, another sad episode in my life as we were very close. She is buried in Milltown Cemetery and I visit her graveside regularly.

The following November Patsy discovered that she was expecting our second child, we had our fingers crossed that he or she would be born a healthy baby. In those days they didn't they hadn't the technology to determine the gender or carry out the various health checks they do now. Come June the following year our prayers were answered as Patsy delivered a lovely baby girl who was healthy in every way. We named her Geraldine. In quick succession came a baby boy whom we named Michael after Patsy's father, followed by Margaret who was named after Patsy's mother, then Henrietta, Denise, Leo, wee Sharon and last but not least our wee Daniel. Five girls and three boys and I have to say, all my kids are lovely and they never gave us much trouble growing up. We moved to Stanhope Drive in Carrick Hill into a three bedroom flat where we stayed for about two years. Just as the troubles broke out we moved across the street into a house, which we later purchased through the tenancy right to buy scheme run by the housing executive. I was still working in the bakery at the time. Patsy's father Michael passed away in the late seventies and her mother Maggie died just twelve days later. Her younger sister Sharon came to live with us but unfortunately she died in her sleep from an epileptic fit. Those were a rough couple of years for us.

When our Hanna left school she got a job in Buntings shirt factory on the Dublin Road which was not far from our house. On the way home from work she would look about to see where I was playing and if she spotted me she would call out.

"It's near your supper time" and me and her would dander home.

Our Hanna would always look out for me. If some bigger lad were to hit me, she would whack them with whatever came to hand, no one was going to hit her Danny as far as Hanna was concerned. All the time we grew up together we never had words, even up until the day she died. I had so much love and respect for her as she was like a big sister to me.

In her late teens she would attend the dance halls such as the Plaza and John Dossers, to name but a few. Then she met her partner for life a man called Michael Ferrin. They married and moved into a house in Andersonstown Gardens where they lived for a few years. Following this they moved to Deanwood Park and they had five lovely children three boys and two girls. There was Geraldine, Paul and Nuala whom I visit regularly, Michael and Jim who is the youngest. Hannah's husband Michael worked as a bookie for his uncle James Murray who owned a bookmakers shop in Wine Tavern Street in Smithfield. Mickey as he was better known to most people also ran a book at the dogs. Aunt Kitty would go up some weekends to babysit. I recall how she loved to sit with a bag of her favourite raspberry ruffles and watch TV. This was a real treat as we had no television down at the Markets. When our Hanna went on her holidays to Butlins in the South of

Ireland she would take Aunt Kitty along to give her a wee bit of a break and also because Aunt Kitty was a great helping hand with the kids.

Our Hannah was blessed with good kids who grew up to make her proud. Her eldest Geraldine went on to become a nurse, she was tall with auburn hair like her mummy. She met and married Robert Dennison who part owned Dennison trucks and she and her family now live in County Kildare. Paul, Hannah's eldest son, went on to own a successful mortgage business in Belfast and was clever enough to bail out before the property boom burst. He now owns a shop called the Money Tree; wish I had a couple of them in the garden. Michael her second eldest son works for an oil company in Singapore as an engineer. He oversees at least two hundred men and never passed his eleven plus. Nuala, her third eldest, lives off the Glen Road in Belfast with her husband Tommy Hughes. Jim Ferrin Hannah's third eldest son is a property developer and lives with his family off the Malone Road in Belfast.

Our Hannah went on to develop rheumatoid arthritis at the age of forty and was crippled with it until the day she died. She passed away seven years ago at the age of seventy one. Her husband Mickey had developed Alzheimer's disease and passed away a few years later. It was terrible to see him wasting away like that especially when you knew him when he was full of life.

He played football at the Oldpark playing fields not far from his home in the Bone. He had a great personality and would tell you stories about football horse racing, boxing, you name it. You could listen to Mickey all night and never get bored.

Chapter 16

Some Old Mates Drinkers And Punters The Lot

I used to have a pint in McGlades bar which ran from Little Donegal St to Upper Donegal St., it was called the Long Bar. I would usually drink with a variety of characters some of them being Patsy's father Michael, Jimmy McCrudden, Johnny Quigley from the New Lodge and Big Tommy McGahan and Jimmy Geoghan both Market men and everyone, of us drinkers and gamblers. McAleavys, bookies was next door, which was in Little Donegal St. We all lived within close proximity to one another and made sure that we all went up home together as they were dangerous times we were living in and it would not have been advisable to dander home alone. You could have been gunned down by a passing car containing loyalist gunmen or picked up by the notorious Shankill Butcher Gang who at the time were targeting any Catholic walking home alone late at night. McElhattons, was another watering hole located in Union St with two bookies beside them namely McAleveys and Sean Grahams. Have you ever noticed that there is always a bookie's within close proximity to a public house. I suppose it's good for business for both concerns. While on the subject of gambling, I must admit that big Tommy McGahan must have been the luckiest punter I have ever met. He would touch for a bet on a regular basis and would not have let you buy a drink from then onwards.

"That's the bookie's money" he would say.

His favourite bet would have been six doubles, four trebles and a quad.

Jim Geoghan told us about an incident that happened when he worked for McGrattan down at the fruit market delivering fruit around the country. On a Friday he would always collect the takings which would usually amount to around three hundred pounds which could be as much as five or six grand now days and he would always hold on to the takings over the weekend and hand them in on a Monday. Jim told us how on this occasion he was passing Duff's Bookie's when he decided to go in and check the results. He told us how his eyes lit on a horse that was priced at twenty five to one on. Gordon

Richards was the jockey on it and Jim thought to himself, if he were to put the takings on this cert thing that it would net him a good week's wages of around twelve pounds or so. Fuck it he thought he'll have the lot on it and go down to Bond St and get his tea before coming back up and collecting his winnings. After all at them odds defeat was utterly impossible, as an American general once said about an upcoming battle. After he got his tea Jim made his way up McCauley St, straight into the bookie's and over to the results board, looking down the sheet expecting to see a large x through his race and a circle around his horse. However it was not there and it was then that the panic set in and his legs turned to jelly at the thought of facing Henry McGrattan on Monday. The horse was beat by a short head but it might as well have been beaten by a hundred miles as far as Jim was concerned, as he reminded us at then time that you can't buy drink and cigarettes with short heads. Jim told us that he couldn't sleep right all that weekend and he made his way round to McGrattan's on Monday morning expecting to be sacked. As Jim entered McGrattan's office, Henry McGrattan was sitting with his back to Jim writing on his desk top when he turned round to face him.

"Just leave the takings on the desk and go down and load up your lorry" said McGrattan.

"Well that's what I've actually come to see you about Mr McGrattan, I lost the money out of my pocket" replied Jim

"Ah fuck! No Jim please don't, tell me that. Now if you had of told me that you lost it in the bookie's I'd buy that. But to think that some monkey has picked it up and probably took his mates out for the weekend and is probably out this very morning for a cure that pisses me off. I think I'll go for a cure I certainly deserve one after receiving that good news on a Monday morning" he said and went straight over to the Royal Bar which was across the street facing the fruit market.

"Do you want me to go over with you Mr McGrattan?" Jim laughed.

"Fuck off Geoghan and go down and load your lorry and I'll be deducting what you owe me from your wages every week until I get all my takings back" replied McGrattan.

McGrattan was later to mention to the yard foreman that he couldn't pay Geoghan off as he was a good grafter and anyhow he needed his money back. Jim had us in stitches telling us that story.

"Would you do the same again" I said to him laughing.

"Not a fucking chance because it took me a month of Sunday's paying it back" said Jim.

Jim passed away a few years back and he surely was one of nature's true gentlemen. His wife Lilly and sons and daughters live not to far from our house and I still have the odd pint or two with his eldest son Paul.

Chapter 17

The Troubles Break Out

The troubles broke out in nineteen sixty nine as a direct consequence of the Unionist Government using bullyboy tactics to suppress the Civil Rights Movement. They broke out first in Derry City before eventually spreading to Belfast and so the nightmare for the people of the North had just began and it hasn't really stopped. In the seventies the kids were that bit older and had grown a little and were always out playing. One Saturday morning my eldest daughter Geraldine came running into the house to inform me that my eldest son Michael had been arrested. There was an Orange Order march heading down Clifton St at the time and as usual Carrick Hill was in lock down with all movement restricted. The Brits and RUC had swamped the area and the soldiers were pointing their weapons towards the local residents. I guess their officers must have briefed them that we were the enemy. I learned that Our Michael had been taken to North Queen St Police Station immediately upon hearing of his arrest I began making my way over to get him but was forced to wait until the Orange parade was over until I was able to cross over the road and make my way towards North Queen St. As I entered the station I gave my name at the front desk and informed the officer on duty that I was here to enquire about the welfare of my fifteen year old son Michael Mulcahy who had been arrested earlier on in the day. He looked at the book in front of him before addressing me.

"Yes Mr Mulcahy we have your son in custody, he's out the back" he said.

"I would like to see him as soon as possible because he is only fifteen years old and could you please tell my why he was arrested? I asked.

"He was arrested for being in possession of an offensive weapon" he said.

"A gun, a knife, a hand grenade what type of weapon may I ask?" said I.

"Oh no nothing as deadly as that" he laughed.

I asked the cop if they were going to charge my fifteen year old son with possession of this so called deadly weapon and he told me that it would be up to the Department of Public Prosecutions as to weather he is charged or not.

"It was a spindle of some old stairway" the officer said.

"Could you please bring my son out so I can take him home to see his mother who is worried sick over all this nonsense. The constable lifted the phone and within a minute in walked our Michael who was accompanied by a female cop who was carrying the so called offensive weapon namely the old wooden spindle which I noticed upon glancing at it that it was riddled with woodworm.

"My God think of all the damage and mayhem you could have caused with such an offensive weapon" I said to our Michael and then I started to get angry.

"So we have hundreds of Orange Men walking down Clifton St with their ceremonial swords, pikes and God knows what else. The army has been deployed and are pointing their weapons towards the defenceless people of Carrick Hill, backed up by well armed RUC squads with armoured plated land rovers and helicopters circling overhead. It's like a scene out of a war movie out there only it's going on as we speak and you people's priority is detaining a fifteen year old kid for possession of a woodworm riddled spindle." I said.

"I am just doing my job here" replied the cop.

"Aye that's what the German SS camp guards said to the Jews as they were loading them into the gas chambers" said I.

I received an angry look for that quote before collecting our Michael from the barracks and heading for home.

Three months later a letter arrived through our letter box and upon opening it I could see from the letter heading that it was a court date for Michael. It read court hearing for Michael Mulcahy scheduled for six weeks time and the charge sheet read Belfast Magistrates Court dated 13. 10. 1981 possessing offensive weapon in a public place. When we attended the court hearing the clerk of the court read out the charges and the judge was presented with the wooden spindle or offensive weapon whatever way you care to look at it and he just shook his head before addressing Michael and asking him to approach the bench. The judge then read out his sentence.

"Michael Mulcahy, I am sentencing you to three months detention in a young offenders centre." I could feel the blood drain from my face. Good God I thought to myself, so this is justice and all for being caught in possession of a piece of wood. Then the judge continued and said that the sentence would be suspended for two years and as you can guess I was more than relieved to hear the suspended bit.

Margaret and Henrietta were in the park, while Michael was out in the street playing with some mates and Geraldine was doing her homework. This one particular night life was going on as normal when all of a sudden all hell broke loose. The loyalists began firing from the hill up at Denmark St in the Lower Shankill into the heart of Carrick Hill. The bullets were tracers, they were white hot and we could see them bouncing around the park. It was complete pandemonium all round, women and children were screaming, Patsy was shouting to me that the kids were in the park, so I ran out and had to get on my hands and knees and crawl along the ground.

There was a perimeter wall which ran along the back of the houses at the end of Stanhope Drive where we lived. The wall stood about six and a half feet tall and all of a sudden the Brits were on the scene and moving towards the wall. They were Royal Marines and not one of them was under, six feet tall. I swear it was like the cavalry to the rescue in the American Wild West. One of the marines jumped up on the bin in our porch beside the wall and started shooting. He must have fired off at least a dozen rounds from his SLR.

"I think I hit one of the bastards" I overheard him say to his mates, the shooting eased off a bit. I then made a bolt for one of the houses near the park where my two kids had been safely kept in someone's house. I was coming back when one of the marines ran down the street and walking backwards in front of us towards the wall next to our house covering us, until we were safely into the house, I must say you have to give credit here where it is due. The loyalist gunmen were continuing to shoot as darkness was beginning to fall and the marines were still shooting back, then under the cover of darkness the loyalists withdrew from their position overlooking Carrick Hill. We later heard that it was the UVF that had perpetrated the attack. You would have to be blinded by bigotry and hatred to have mounted an operation of this kind targeting innocent women and children, the people from Carrick Hill who never had any intention of attacking anyone.

I woke on Wednesday morning at five o'clock on a mild August morning. I had to get ready for work as my shift started at six thirty and Patsy and the children were still fast asleep, so I made myself a bit of breakfast the put on my coat and stepped outside closing the door easily behind me. It was dry and mild and the dawn was breaking, as I was making my way down to Inglis bakery and I noticed there were other people making their way to work just like I was and the buses were actually running on time for a change. I walked down Donegal St and onto Victoria St and as I got to May St I seen these army lorry's coming from the direction of Oxford St. They were probably coming from the docks and I stopped and waited to cross the road which seemed like an eternity, as the lorry's just kept coming and they were going in all directions. Little did I realise it at the time but internment without trial was about to be introduced and I was witnessing history in the making that would have far reaching consequences mainly for the Catholic Community.

After the last lorry passed by I made my way across Cromac Square and on to Inglis bakery in Eliza St and straight to the locker room and then the score room. When I eventually arrived at my work station I could see that big Gerry Reynolds who was Skinny's brother was already there, waiting for me. Gerry was to be my work mate that week and we were plating the trays of proofed dough into the oven. I told Gerry about the army lorries and how I thought they were going to a variety of army barracks all over the country due to the fact that they were travelling in all different directions. At around nine thirty the word came in that internment had broken out and that they were lifting hundreds of men in and around the Catholic/ Nationalist working class districts throughout the Belfast area. This was why the army lorries were travelling in all directions, I thought to myself. There was mayhem throughout the North. Hundreds of innocent men were dragged from their beds and thrown into the back of an army lorry. If they professed their innocence they would be assaulted and many of them received terrible beatings. Some doors were kicked in only to find they were looking for people who had deceased years earlier. I believe they must have used street directories and just picked the names at random. They lifted around seven hundred men in total, some were as young as seventeen while others were in their sixties and the lives of some of these men would never be the same again. We later learned that the internees were transported to a number of various holding centres located throughout the North, Crumlin Road Jail, Armagh jail, and the Maidstone prison ship. They would later be transferred to the Long Kesh prison camp which was near completion.

Everything was going as planned for the British Government as it was part of their agenda to expect a violent response and they certainly got one. Cars buses and vans were set alight, business premises were torched, barricades were erected in Nationalist estates across the city as the resident's tried to put up some sort of resistance, in other words all hell broke loose.

We plated up the last batch of bread on the oven at nine o'clock that fateful morning to allow the work force, especially those of them who lived in other parts of the city to get home safely. On my way home I made my way round to Cromac Square where there was crowds of men gathering and standing on the roads and footpaths and you could tell that there was trouble brewing around the streets of the Market's area that morning. As I stood talking to a couple of fellows I knew, I noticed a guy standing opposite me whom I had never seen around before and he was suited and booted with collar and tie. As two R.U.C. land rovers drove into Cromac Square he turned to the crowd and shouted in a Belfast accent.

"There's the razzers."

Taken aback I thought to myself now that's a name I have never heard before. I was wondering was he Special Branch but then thought naw because he wouldn't have said razzers, cops or peelers yes but not razzers. He then pointed towards Geordie Stone's bicycle repair shop which was situated beside Eileen's fish and chip shop.

"They are Protestants aren't they" I heard him say

"So what about it, a persons religion is their own business and no one else's" I butted in

Geordie Stone had lived in the Market's area for as long as I can remember and I knew his son Raymond who worked in the shop with his father. I often wonder did this character think for one second that the crowd would rush over and burn Geordie's shop to the ground and then attack the razzers as he called them on his command and if so he was badly mistaken because that was never going to happen. In hindsight looking back on this episode I firmly believe that this guy was in all likelihood an M.I.5 field officer trying to escalate the conflict to suit their own agenda and they were probably over on the loyalist side doing the same thing.

What had brought this situation about was the eighty years of oppression the Catholic/Nationalist Community had to endure under the old Stotmont apartheid style Government. The first Stormont Unionist Government which was formed after partition came into power on the seventh of June nineteen twenty one and was led by the notorious bigot Sir James Craig who would rule with an iron fist. One of his sidekicks was a man named Charlie Londonderry who, in the early thirties, invited a top Nazi called Ribbentrop over from Germany to see for himself how the Stormont Government handled the Catholic minority in the North of Ireland. Who gave this moron the authority to invite this Nazi scum over to contaminate my land with his filth is beyond me. It was not long after his return to Germany that the holocaust started against the Jewish people, innocent men, women and children were hauled off to the gas chambers and the ovens and the rest is history.

Craig was also instrumental in introducing the Special Powers Act in nineteen twenty two which imposed such laws as the death penalty for possession of arms and authorized flogging for certain offences such as carrying a republican news sheet. Trial by jury was suspended and coroners inquests were abolished from nineteen twenty two onwards as Craig's Government effectively operated a policy of terrorism directed against the Catholic and Nationalist people. A policy of turning a blind eye to unionist mobs aided by Craig's own special constabulary known as the B Specials carrying out burnings looting and evictions were the order of the day in nineteen twenty two. Twenty three thousand people were driven from their homes and nearly five hundred people were killed and almost two thousand wounded during the course of that year. History would then repeat itself later in the century when under a similar Unionist Government the same thing would happen in the late sixties and early seventies until even the British Government had to admit that these morons were unfit to govern.

Chapter 18

The Partition Of Ireland

Whilst living in London Charlie Londonderry befriended a certain attractive American socialite one Lady Hazel Lavery who was in her late thirties at the time some twenty years younger than her husband the world renowned artist Sir John Lavery who hailed from Belfast's own Donegal St. His people were wine merchants and he was baptized in St Patrick's Church , where you will still see Lady Hazel's portrait which he gifted to the chapel. When you enter the front doors of the chapel and turn left you can see the painting which portrays Lady Hazel as Our Lady of The Lakes holding two young children by the hands.

Lady Hazel would be instrumental in getting Michael Collins to sign the treaty with Britain. I firmly believe she was a British agent, the British Mata Hari from the word go and I could not believe Collins allowed himself to be duped in such a way by this woman, a man with his experience in the field of intelligence.

In Dublin during the Anglo Irish war of independence Collins decimated Britain's network of spies in the city but in London it was a different situation where British intelligence held sway in their own turf. As soon as big Mick set eyes on Hazel Lavery at their first meeting, he was hooked, everything was going according to plan for the Brits, get Collins to sign and all the rest would follow suit. De Valera had previously had five meetings with Lloyd George the then liberal leader and British Prime Minister prior to the treaty signing. I believe De Valera was rattled by the Welsh Wizard as Lloyd George was termed then and decided that he wasn't going to face Lloyd George at the treaty negotiations table and for that reason sent Collins not to destroy him as some have suggested but thinking that Collins was the man to bring back a republic. I believe De Valera believed himself that firey Mick would be more than a match for the Welsh Wizard and maybe he was right but was Collins a match for Lady Hazel? I doubt it very much. The Brits did not want De Valera at the negotiation table in my view due to the fact that he was a family man with a strong devotion to the catholic faith which they believed would make it more difficult for them to enable him to strike up a relationship with Hazel Lavery or as it might otherwise be called the honey trap. It was Mick who was the single man that they wanted all along and that's why they got Lloyd

George to give De Valera such a hard time. The letters that Hazel Lavery received from Collins went straight to British intelligence who would read them before forwarding them on. After the signing of the treaty with Britain, Hazel Lavery was to travel to Ireland to join Collins when the civil war broke out and probably for the purpose of keeping tabs on the progress. Mick was involved in the war with the anti treaty forces and the Brits were hoping he would bring it to an early conclusion.

Lady Lavery stated in her memoirs that whilst staying with Collins at one of the Dublin hotels that he ranted that he was so fed up with civil war and watching his friends die needlessly that he invited her to go to America with him but that she declined his offer. Collins would later be shot and killed in his homeland in West Cork at a place called Beal Na Blath just outside of Clonakility. As his body was being transported back to Dublin to lie in State the cortege passed through a small village where it is said they stopped and sent for a priest to administer the last rites and when the priest seen the body in the coffin he turned on his heels and briskly walked away. At this point one of the young Free State soldiers lifted his rifle and took aim with the intention of shooting the priest when Emmet Dalton grabbed the barrel of the rifle and pulled it from the young soldier, such was the feeling at the time in the South West of Ireland with the signing of the treaty. It later emerged Emmet Dalton was indeed an MI6 agent. Michael Collins stated at the time that the signing of the treaty was freedom to gain freedom, what nonsense. As for the Catholic/Nationalist people of the North of Ireland it was freedom to gain ninety years of oppression as far as they were concerned.

General Laim Lynch the general commanding the Anti Treaty forces during the Irish Civil War was quoted as saying.

"We fought for an Irish Republic and I will not live under any other law."

He would later lose his life fighting against the Free State Forces in the Knockmealdown Mountains and he was just twenty nine years old at the time. At the height of the Civil War he did everything in his power to avert a split in the army and it probably cost him the victory in the conflict. He fought alongside Tom Barry in and around County Cork. Tom Barry was a commander of genius in Cork who fought against the British Empire during the War of Independence and his many running battles with the British are legendary. Men like Dick Barret, Laim Deasey and Tom Hales, to name but a few would have followed Barry through hell and high water and they did just that. They formed themselves into the famous Flying Columns which moved around the countryside attacking the enemy wherever and whenever the opportunity presented itself with speed and proficiency and it didn't matter to Barry how numerous the enemy forces were on the field of battle. Barry knew that his military tactics and the bravery of his men would rout The Brits wherever they showed their hand. With virtually few weapons, and with most of what weaponry they did possess having come from what was retrieved from their fallen enemy, these Irish Men from all over the Southern Counties and further a field brought the war to the British Forces of Occupation. Following centuries of British Oppression these men were honed into a seasoned fighting force. Many people believe that it was the actions of Barry and his Flying Columns that forced the hand of the mighty British Empire to negotiate the peace terms

The Civil War suited the Brits agenda perfectly because they could now manipulate the situation by deploying their widely used tactic of the divide and conquer rule comes to mind here. Do I blame Collins here? Well yes and no. I believe Mick should have fulfilled his duty as an Irish Republican and refused to sign the British Treaty instead of allowing his judgement to be clouded by his love and passion for Hazel Lavery. On the other hand he had to contend with British treachery and they after all are the masters of treachery deception and intrigue. Their intelligence services are second to none and the Honey Trap springs to mind here. They have used it to great effect down through the years and the name of Kitty O'Shea comes to mind here. Kitty O'Shea's affair with the Irish politician Charles Stewart Parnell who was a thorn in the side of the British Establishment would eventually lead to the popular politician's resignation due to the scandal it created. Kitty was the wife of a British Army Officer at the time. The Lavery's were accepted members of British High Society and the timing couldn't have suited the Brits better. It was an ideal move for them at the time of the treaty negotiations and who better to have on your side than Sir John Lavery and with his Irish connections and his beautiful Wife Hazel, who's job it was to befriend Big Mick Collins.

After Mick Collins's death the lovely Lady Hazel took up with Kevin O'Higgens, who was seen then as the Irish Mussolini who was the Minister for Justice at the time. O'Higgens signed the execution order for seventy seven IRA, Volunteers which included four of the organizations leaders and the man who served as his own Best Man at his wedding Rory O'Connor was executed in December 1922. O'Higgen's was handing out execution orders like they were going out of fashion quoting the old saying when the oppressed become the oppressor and most of these executions would have been carried out by my name sake Richard Mulcahy. He also stated that the Catholic population of the North should endorse the treaty and accept that the six occupied counties shall remain under British rule. Now that might have suited O'Higgens who was living safely down in Dublin a hundred miles away where he and his family wouldn't have to run the gauntlet from their burning home chased by sectarian Orange Mobs. He also for saw his own death when he stated

"Nobody who has did, what I have did, can expect to live a long life."

Later on his prophecy would come to fruition when he was gunned down by two Anti- Treaty men while making his way to Sunday Mass without his bodyguards. Lady Hazel Lavery said that she actually hated the man (Kevin O'Higgens) which, leaves one thinking, why was she associating with him in the first place. I can only assume that it was at the behest of MI6, to make sure the Civil War was brought to a speedy conclusion in favour of the Pro Treaty Forces. In future years Lady Hazel's portrait would appear on the Irish Punt believe it or not portrayed as an Irish Colleen, when in actual fact she was a British Agent who was instrumental in destroying The Irish Nation. My God Ireland's Hero's would turn over in their graves at the thought of it.

I often wonder did Collins and the Pro Treaty crowd really believe that when the last Wee Tommy climbed aboard the troop ship as the Brits were pulling out of the twenty six counties singing pack up your troubles in your old kit bag, that they had seen the last of them. The British Tommy's may have departed from these shores but the men in the pinstripe suits with their briefcases would stay behind and dictate policy from behind the scenes for whatever government that came to power. No matter what policies were put forward they would make sure that it was in their interests and also that of big business. When the delegation who were negotiating the treaty, learned that the six counties were not up for discussion they should have lifted their brief cases and headed for the nearest exit. What we were left with was ninety years of oppression, with discrimination in employment and housing widespread and the gerrymandering of the political process. There was no such thing as one man one vote or political progress in fact there was no political anything and Catholics were treated as second class citizens in all aspects of life. In fact the Anti Catholic pogroms were the order of the day when Catholics were shot down on the streets and burned out of their houses by the thousands. The leading Home Ruler J P O'Kane wrote that far from being an impulsive outbreak of violence, the pogroms were actually a well planned design with a specific ambition. The poor Catholics in the artificial Unionist State had their rights trampled over and achieving a United Ireland was the last thing on the mind of the ordinary Catholic unless they happened to be a republican when the treaty was signed. The Irish Prime Minister Laim Cosgrave closed the border saying that he was fed up with war, now what a stupid statement to make and a cowardly one at that. It obviously didn't matter to Cosgrave that his fellow Irishmen, women and children would have to suffer at the hands of an oppressive Unionist Government for the next ninety years. At that time Cahir Healey a Nationalist Leader who was interned on the prison ship Agenta which was moored up in Derry wrote to the Southern Government asking them if there was any way they could afford to give some help to the hard pressed Nationalist People of The North. Sadly he later wrote in his diary

"I am afraid we will have to look after ourselves."

Chapter 19

The Creation And Maintenance Of An Artificial State

Craig the first Prime minister of the Northern Government whose infamous quote was a Protestant Parliament for a Protestant People was the leader of the Unionist Party and an out and out bigot. Basel Brooke who was to become Prime Minister in later years was also quoted as saying that he would not have one about the place or in his employ when asked his opinion of Catholics. The Unionist Party became known as the nod and a wink party. They never wrote down or logged any sectarian statements. They found out that a gentleman working in the grounds of the Parliament Buildings at Stormont, was a Catholic and he promptly received his walking papers. Apparently this man had served with distinction during the Second World War and got the post due to his having a letter of recommendation from a high ranking officer in the British Army but that didn't save him. A telephonist up at Stormont was also a Catholic and would become their next target as they were concerned that she might be listening to their conversations so she also had to go. After the subversives were found and rounded up men were seen searching the grounds and the corridors and under the floor boards with Anti Catholic search detectors, they weren't taking any chances. The Stormont Cabinet held an emergency meeting to discuss the grave situation as to how two Catholic's got by their Anti Catholic radar system and it was decided to apply more stringent measures to deal with the crisis. That night Basil Brooke was to get a good night's sleep in the knowledge that no more Catholics would be anywhere near the grounds of Stormont. If you let one in through the doors he said to a close friend the next thing you know there are hundreds of them.

In the mid fifties Basil embarked on a journey on his yacht to America to try and find some work for his Protestant Workforce. After travelling around various parts of America with no success on the jobs front he entered a car factory and was shown around the place. The floor manager then took Basil into his office.

"Well, what do you think of our Cadillac's?" He said to Basil in his American accent which sounds very much like Catholic's.

"I wouldn't have one about the place" says Basil and at that the manager showed him the door and slammed it shut behind him, so poor old Basil had to sail back to Belfast with no work for the boys. I guess academic qualifications weren't a priority and the lack of such would certainly not prevent a man from taking his place in the Unionist Cabinet of the day as the only essential requirement sought for such a high position was Anti Catholic bigotry. When Basil eventually docked at Belfast the press were waiting for him but he refused to leave his cabin. However Basil wasn't the only bigot to serve at Stormont. Even the moderate Unionist who was Minister of Education under Sir James Craig, Lord Charlemont displayed a contempt for Catholic's in general when he told an advocate for better community relations in the 1930's.

"Look at Joe Devlin, these people have cunning, but that's all."

It was his opinion that Northern Catholic's regardless of class or education were rarely fit to hold public office.

He would turn over in his grave if he could see them now. These rich power hungry morons couldn't care less about their own working class Protestant people who are the salt of the earth in many cases May Blood being a perfect example, I wish there were a lot more like May. Anyhow these morons used the Protestant working classes to keep themselves in power. They should have called it the bigotry institution for they destroyed generations of our people down through the years with their policy of denying our people skilled labour and trades. If they had of taken our people into a power sharing government when the state was founded I doubt there would have been any trouble in the late sixties and seventies.

A few years down the line and Captain Terence O'Neill took over the helm as Prime Minister. His famous quote was.

"If you give a Catholic a job, a house and a TV he will live like a good Protestant."

I've often wondered was it a coloured TV but anyhow what a blatantly sectarian statement to make. O'Neill's then Minister of Home Affairs Brian Faulkner would later become Prime Minister and would be responsible for the introduction of internment without trial. Catholic men were beaten and tortured and in some instances were thrown from helicopters blindfolded believing themselves to be over the rooftops when in fact they were only a few feet of the ground, psychological torture at it's best. Faulkner's infamous quote at the time was to say that they were squealing like rats. The same man a couple of years down the line was out fox hunting when he fell from his horse and broke his neck.

In the early sixties The Stormont Government allowed the Old Nationalist Party to set up shop and become the opposition party and what a laugh as it was just a ploy to give the Unionist Government a bit of respectability around the world. The Nationalist Party was led by a guy called Eddie McAteer who hailed from Derry and the majority of its members came from within the ranks of the Ancient Order of Hibernians who held parades every year around the country. Why? You may ask and to be truthful your guess is as good as mine for there was no way they were going to unseat this Apartheid Party for this was one of the most oppressive governments in the Western Hemisphere if not the world with their Special Powers Legislation the envy of South Africa's Apartheid System. The Special Powers Act was mainly directed at the Catholic Nationalist population and should you be unlucky enough to be caught in possession of a republican news sheet, you could be arrested and flogged and kept in for as long as the State deemed possible. You could also be arrested on the word of a police officer without any charges being brought against you and the police ranks were one hundred percent Unionist and ninety five percent Protestant.

The Unionist Army of around ten thousand included members of the RUC, the A and B Specials, CID and Special Branch were all geared up to facilitate the State. Life wasn't easy in them days being a Catholic but then it wasn't easy being a boy named Sue either. The British Government introduced direct rule in 1972 like the second coming of Cromwell and our nightmare began all over again. They espoused that they were here only as peacekeepers to keep the two communities apart but what utter nonsense that was. Who do you think started the trouble in the first place only the Brits of course with their policy of divide and conquer. In the majority of conflicts around the globe there is always the coup d'etat ready to overthrow a government and the students usually end up on the streets first. I firmly believe that the powers that be in Westminster were planning their response in the dark corridors of power long before the events took place. Remember the Peoples Democracy Movement and the Civil Rights marchers who were shot down by British Paratroopers on the streets of Derry resulting in thirteen fatalities. Then we had the Ballymurphy Massacre that took place during the internment purge that claimed the lives of eleven innocent civilians including a Catholic Priest who was going to the aid of an injured man. These incidents cleared the streets of protesters and this enabled the Brits to engage in a shooting war with the various Republican groups and opened the way for their counter insurgents, the Loyalist assassins to get a clear run. I believe one of the main reasons they came over was to undermine Harold Wilson, the then Prime Minister who was leader of the Labour Party and would have been viewed by the power brokers as a left winger. I also believe that they welcomed the opportunity to dissolve the Stormont Apartheid Government which in my opinion they would have viewed as a stumbling block to peace and reconciliation years down the line. The Brits don't do things on the spur of the moment, they plan years ahead and the conflict here in the North also presented them with the opportunity to oil their war machine which had been lying dormant for a few years for future campaigns further a field. Talk about neighbours from hell that's an understatement.

Raiding parties, doors being kicked in, helicopters hovering overhead night and day, drive by shootings carried out by loyalist gunmen with help from collusion within the forces of the State and army undercover units, bombings and army foot patrols walking the streets that would eventually become invisible as you got used to seeing them each and every day. We have had our share of killings in this wee part of our country, Bloody Sunday, Bloody Friday, the Ballymurphy Massacre, McGurks Bar and the ten Republican Hunger Strikers who would not be criminalized and would die for their beliefs, I could go on and on. After three and a half thousand deaths and tens of thousands injured and thousands more banged up in jails from both sides of the divide the question must be asked. Surely there must be an answer to all this

When the troubles broke out in 1969 the great Belfast linen industry had long since died and the ship building industry was in decline or should I say free fall. Yeah sure we had some potato fields, a couple of dulse factories and oh aye just in case I forget a potted herring factory and as the troubles raged on the place soon became an industrial wasteland. I can remember watching the film the Magnificent Seven where you had Yule Brynner standing over Elli Wallace as he was dying on the ground and Wallace says.

"You came back, but why? Men like you for a place like this why? There is nothing here but a few bean fields."

To me it reminded me of the futility of the war here and the waste of life and limb and for what. We were struggling, all our lives just to make ends meet and fend for our families and then to be drawn into another conflict, how could this be, we never wanted to attack anyone. In the book A Very British Jihad the author Paul Larkin stated that by 1973 the British State had introduced into Ireland its standard counter insurgency kit which it had developed in the Empire during the post war era. The army with their military intelligence units, MI6, MI5, the RUC and their Special Branch and the Ulster Defence Regiment were all jostling for position in this tiny little patch and they were all deployed against an enemy who's territory consisted of a couple of housing estates and a strip along the border with the twenty six counties.

In the summer of 1966 Big Ian Paisley the founder of the DUP along with hundreds of his followers and backed up by the RUC and B Specials were making their way down the Ravenhill Road towards Cromac Square in the Markets. They were on their way to the Presbyterian Assembly Buildings in Howard Street to confront the leader of the Presbyterian Church, the Rev Bishop Runcie who had invited a member of the Catholic Hierarchy to address the assembly. Just as Paisley and his mob with their union jacks and banners fluttering in the wind approached Cromac Square they were confronted by a counter demonstration from the Markets. As angry exchanges ensued the police drew their batons and all hell broke loose. Fighting broke out between the Market's men and the police and Paisley's crowd broke ranks and headed off in the direction of May St leaving the Market's men and the cops to fight it out between them. More police reinforcements arrived on the scene and this resulted in mass arrests of the Market's men who suffered most at the hands of the RUC who used their batons to crush all resistance to their iron clad rule. The Market's men who got arrested were to appear in court the following day and some of them would eventually be given a six month sentence for disorderly behaviour. It must have been hard on some of these men that were never in trouble before being banged up in a jail and separated from their families and loved ones. Paisley was eventually arrested a few weeks later as the Government took a red face with embarrassment. Mr Paisley was to bestow a great honour on the Market's people when he compared them to Apaches, the great American Indian Tribe whose guerrilla tactics and running battles with The US Calvary were legendry. Thank God it appears that the Market's area is now free from having to witness them bigoted sectarian marches parading through the streets.

Aunt Kitty told me that in the 1930's the Orange Lodge used to parade around May's Market and over the Queen's Bridge towards East Belfast. I can recall Aunt Kitty telling about one instance when an Orange Parade was beaten out of the Market's when they retreated down Keegan St with their swords and their pikes.

It came about when someone threw a paving stone, which we called a kidney paver back in the day and it went straight through one of the Marchers drums and all hell broke loose. Fighting broke out and as they got to Staunton St the people ran out of their houses and beat the Orange mob back with anything they could lay their hands on, floor brushes. Shovels, buckets filled with water, cups, plates and bricks. The Orange Mob retreated up Stewart St and that was the end of that for they never ventured down that path again. They used top walk down the Ormeau Road year in and year out until shortly after the tragedy at Sean Graham's bookmakers where five innocent people were slaughtered by loyalist assassin's. During the next Orange March that paraded down the Ormeau Road after the tragic event one of the marchers lifted their hand and put up five fingers referring to the five innocent victims that had been murdered. Two of the perpetrators of this heinous bookies attack were later killed themselves in an IRA attack, If you live by the sword so shall you die by the sword comes to mind here.

Chapter 20

Some Welcome Respite In Falcarragh And Omeath

The troubles were still raging with the shootings and the bombings continuing on a daily basis and the chapel was organizing for families to go down south for their own safety. Patsy's mother Maggie pleaded with her after the latest shooting incident near our home, to take the four children and make her way down south. A lot of families from other parts of Belfast would also make the journey and they were later to be called the northern refugees. Maggie Davis also sent Patsy's sisters and youngest brother Seamus to give her a hand. They put her up in a four bedroom house in Falcarragh beside the Atlantic Ocean on Co Donegal's North Coast. After I finished work at the weekends I would often make my way down on the bus to see Patsy and the kids. It was a picturesque village surrounded by mountains as far as the eye could see and for the most part the weather was great. The children were enjoying themselves and on occasions I would take them to some of the local beaches that were something else with the pure white sand that stretched for mile after mile. Patsy said she felt a lot safer for her and the kids and every Saturday I was up Patsy and I would go into the village to one of the many public houses that ran along the main street. When you entered the bar all eyes were upon you, probably thinking that's them poor refugees from the north. We would go and take a seat at one of the many tables and when I would go up to order a drink, the locals in the bar would nod in your direction. I could overhear them talking in Irish but that was way out of my league. Although we were taught Irish at school most of the lads including myself were not interested. Maybe if they had have taught us Irish history in school we might have shown more interest in learning our native tongue.

Come Monday morning I would awake early to get the bus back home as I was scheduled to start work at three o'clock in the afternoon, back to porridge as they would say. The kids were still in bed sleeping as I got my breakfast and after saying goodbye to Patsy and telling her that I planned to come back up next weekend, I headed for the bus station. I boarded the bus at eight thirty and headed to Derry for the change over and eventually arrived in Belfast around twelve thirty. On my way from the bus station to my home in Carrick Hill I stopped of and bought myself a newspaper. The headlines were the usual doom and gloom of people being shot dead on the street, car bombs going off and more Catholic's getting burned out of their houses, it was not good reading I can tell you. It seemed to be escalating and I thought to myself, what the hell are the Brits up to here. I headed round to Patsy's mother's house where she had a bit of dinner ready for me.

"I'm getting our Patsy a caravan in Omeath" she said before adding.

"The children can spend the summer holidays there away from the troubles."

Omeath was a little sleepy village nestling at the foot of the Cooley Mountains on the southern shore of Carlingford Lough with superb views of the Mourne Mountains on the northern side of the Lough. Omeath was just 4 miles from the border as some people would call it, however it would sound better if the word artificial were placed before border anyhow it was only fifty minutes journey from Carrick Hill and that would suit us just fine. Patsy and the kids came home from Donegal after three weeks as she was expecting our fifth child, who we would eventually name Denise and once again we were blessed with the birth of a healthy child and thank God for it. Patsy's mother eventually purchased the caravan in Omeath and when the school holidays came along Patsy would take our five children including our new arrival young baby Denise off to Omeath for the summer holidays and what about poor Dan? Well I was able to enjoy it on the odd weekend. Patsy's father Michael would run them down to Omeath in his car and once you got to Newry it was only ten minutes away and I can remember Patsy telling me she loved reaching Newry as the children had her tortured by asking every five minutes

"Are we nearly there yet Mammy."

I would arrive down the following day and always loved the welcoming bowl of stew I received on arrival. The father in law would always bring down a large pot of stew that Patsy's mother had made up the night before and just needed to be warmed up due to the fact that it had been cooked the previous night. We would unpack the suitcases and have our tea and then the children would go down to the beach to play, as the caravan was literally situated on the beachfront, it was heaven on earth as far as I was concerned. Patsy would always keep a close eye on the children as she was a bit over protective and wouldn't let them out of their sight.

Michael the father in law and myself would make our way down to the pup for a couple of pints of Guinness and believe me the Guinness in Omeath was something else compared to Belfast. Apparently it was a couple of percent stronger in the south as opposed to the north. After consuming a pint or two Michael and I made our way back to the caravan, where Patsy had a large pot of stew warmed up and ready to eat, the kids were already at the table and it went down a treat. After a couple of hours Patsy's father left to return home. On Sunday morning I took the four children Geraldine, Michael, Margaret and Henrietta down to Carlingford which is about four miles outside Omeath to give Patsy a break with baby Denise. There were amusements there for the kids to play on and I got them ice cream and something to eat. I took them to see the sailing ships and there was also a medieval parade and the locals were in fancy dress. The weather was fine and sunny and there was a good crowd down that Sunday.

I met Norman Wetherall from the Markets with his wife Marie and their two kids amongst the crowd and he told me that he was down looking for a caravan to buy for the family. We went into one of the many bars that lined the small streets of Carlingford and had a couple of pints. We talked about work and the most recent events of the troubles and I told him that as soon as I heard of one of the caravans coming up for sale that he would be the first to know. As it happened, Patsy's brother Roy Davis and his wife Margaret, who had a caravan down a bit from ours on the same site were looking to upgrade to a larger one. The one they had was only a two berth caravan and they now had three kids and even though you could convert the living room couch into an extra bed they still wanted to upgrade. A month later, Roy bought a six berth caravan down at Giles's Quay not far from

Carlingford. I informed Norman Wetherall that Roy was selling his caravan which he then went and bought. Norman and I would travel up and down from Omeath to work in his car and every weekend when we hit Omeath we would all pile into Howe's bar. On the odd occasion we would have the kids with us so it wouldn't be a late one. We would drink with Paddy McMahon or Fish as we nicknamed him and his wife Anne who was a lovely woman that sadly has since passed away, also Harry and Tommy Fisher and Teddy Fields who has also died and his wife Consetta were also Omeath regulars.

Chapter 21

Dan Mulcahy Versus Usain Bolt

I was for the most part on the evening shift at Inglis, working in the plain bread section, working from three o'clock in the afternoon until eleven o'clock that night and it seemed then like all I did at the time was work and sleep. You would see the kids for about an hour in the morning before they went to school and then would not see them again until the following morning. If you worked in the cooler where the bread was cooled down, sliced, wrapped and then packed on to wooden trays, you would start at one o'clock in the morning and work until seven o'clock in the morning. That was the graveyard shift and Skinny Reynolds used to always say that the graveyard shift was for peelers and brass nails. Jimmy Moss and I would sometimes mop the floors in the plain bread section and after mopping one side I would say to him.

"Are you not going to dry the tiles?"

"The fucking air will dry them" he would quirk up talking out the side of his mouth as usual. His brothers Davy and Bow Moss also worked in the plain bread section and Davy was a real character who in later years would be complaining about suffering from gout.

"That's too much rich food you are eating" I would say to him.

"Rich food my fuck, pasty suppers is all I eat" he would laugh.

One Sunday morning in August in the late seventies I was heading down to work at Inglis bakery. It was around eight o'clock in the morning and it was a beautiful sunny day and I wasn't out drinking that Saturday night, just as well as there were a few people hurrying to eight o'clock mass. I was making my way down Donegal St and as I passed the News Letter Office I noticed that there was this car driving up Lower Donegal St on the right hand side and as the car drew level the guy who was driving pointed a gun in my direction. Not waiting around to see who he was pointing at I went into full flight and the car did a u turn and came after me. Now I recon that the distance from the Newsletter Office to the bottom of Donegal St would be around one hundred yards or so and I believe I could have passed Usian Bolt on the way down. When your life is in danger like that adrenalin takes over and statistics go out the window. As I flew down towards Warring St they fired a shot at me but thank God they missed. I was waiting for the car to draw level but believe it or not they decided to drive towards East Bridge St as Warring St was one way. They then drove onto High St and by that time I had flew up Skipper St and across to where the Albert Clock stood and ran up Victoria St. I looked back at the car as it drove by the Albert Clock and noticed the driver putting his arm out the window and shaking his fist probably meaning you lucky bastard. I ran on down Victoria St towards May St just in case they had decided to drive down Oxford St and cut me off and there was no sign of them but I kept running anyhow. As I got to Cromac Square and slowed down I realized why they did not drive past Ann St because they would have had to pass by Musgrave St Barracks. The old game of Rallyo came into its own thinking back, when in my school days I used to run for hours on end. To me this didn't appear to be a planned hit but more of an opportunist meeting as they drove up Lower Donegal St and spotted me on my way to work, they probably thought that I was coming from St Patrick's Chapel seeing as I was coming from that direction. These trained loyalist killers were backed up by army reconnaissance units who on many occasions cleared the way for them to murder innocent Catholics and also aided their getaway.

I made my way on round to Inglis bakery never as glad to see work in all my life, the sweat was lashing out of me and after changing into my whites I went straight up the plain bread department to and started work. I never told anyone about my ordeal and I know some other people would have gone round to the pub to get themselves a stiff drink but it never really had any lasting effect on me. Although I do remember it from time to time I had a family to look after and of course Sunday was double time and I couldn't feed my kids by sitting in some pub. When I finished my shift around six o'clock, I made my way home up May St, past the City Hall, along Royal Avenue and up North St where there were plenty of people around. All the way up to Carrick Hill and I was still looking over my shoulder from time to time. Patsy and the children where having their supper when I got home and for my part, I was just so glad to be coming home to my family at all as many a one wasn't so lucky. That night after they had finished their supper and were going to bed I would hug all my kids a little tighter. I never told Patsy what had happened that morning as in doing so I know that she would be worrying each and every morning when I went out to work. However I would tell her about it a few years later.

Thank God for the Good Friday Agreement, as now you don't have to look over your shoulder for passing cars or your door getting kicked in and getting shot by loyalist assassins under the direction of British Army Intelligence through the now proven collusion that was ongoing at the time. Now days I wouldn't be able to run as fast as I did back then, in fact my running days are well and truly over as I now have a bad back maybe its something to do with age. Catholics had to run all their lives since this artificial state was set up from their burning homes with their wee bundles of belongings under their arms and their young children crying and running beside them from

Orange mobs and their counterpart in the British Police Force the RUC. When the Brits introduced direct rule in the early seventies there was no Catholic middle class just the rich and the poor and unfortunately I was in the latter category. They brought over Laing's the builders an English firm who employed Catholic contractors who in turn employed Catholic workers. Castle Court was a prime example and more large projects followed.

I can recall one morning during the early seventies and it was a week day and my kids were all fast asleep as it was early and they had a few hours kip left before they needed to get up for school. It was about five o'clock in the morning and I was getting up as I always did at that time for work when I heard all this drilling going on. I thought it might have been the water board fixing the water mains so I went to the door only to discover that it was the British Army who was doing the drilling. They were installing metal angle up rights with barbed wire between them across Stanhope St leading onto Clifton St. Apparently they were to prevent car bombs from leaving Catholic estates for the purpose of blowing up the town centre. The people in Carrick Hill could barely make a living never mind blowing up the town. The kids were woken out of their sleep but I got them back to bed and went down the stairs to light the fire. I turned on the television and the news was reporting that operation Motor Man had began after being introduced by the then Secretary of State for Northern Ireland William Whitelaw. Now Willy was the first politician to take up this role following the introduction of direct rule but he certainly would not be the last. A number of years after Willy came a fellow by the name of, Merlyn Rees who attempted to criminalize the republican prisoners in the H Blocks of Long Kesh and he himself was succeeded by the Rhinestone Cowboy that was Roy Mason. Mason came here dressed in his wee safari suit with his shorts, boots and pipe and the only thing missing was the elephant gun between his arms like a miniature Stewart Granger or should I say Farley Granger as he was to leave here as a Farley's rusk. Brian Feeny who was a respected journalist who wrote for the Irish News stated that Roy Mason was the stupidest Secretary of State to ever take up the post here. In saying that few British politicians relished the chance to take up the post of Secretary of State for Northern Ireland and it would serve as an outpost for many a cabinet minister who had fallen from grace and been demoted.

John Stalker and Sir John Stephens were both assigned to investigate different aspects of the troubles here. John Stalker investigated the shoot to kill policy and Sir John Stephens investigated the activities of the loyalist death squads and the collusion that existed between them and the British Intelligence Services. Just as both men were getting somewhere near the truth they were discredited. It began with the sinister burning of Sir John Stephen's offices and continued with the framing of John Stalker, in which it was claimed he took backhanders from a shady underworld figure. These allegations were proven to be totally unfounded. I firmly believe that both these men, were men of integrity, who as police officers would perform their duty to the highest standard and would have went to the ends of the earth and left no stone unturned to solve a crime no matter who the perpetrators were. If the Brits thought for one second that these two men would have done a whitewash job then they were badly mistaken. Sir John Stephens, during one of his stays here was to quote how in his opinion the British actually kept the war going on for longer than was really necessary and that they could have brought it to a conclusion long before they did. Later on both men were to resign from the force.

Chapter 22

More Additions To The Clan And Life Resumes As Normal

Three more additions were added to the Mulcahy Clan soon after Denise, They were Leo, Sharon and Wee Daniel. I remember thinking to myself I'll need three jobs from here on in, and the days of wine and roses will have to go as well as the wee flutter in the bookie's. I might as well go into a monastery or do a runner. Fuck it I'll get another job or just put Patsy out to work only joking.

Ninteen seventy four was the world cup year and Laim McGuire and I backed Holland and they were eventually beaten in the final. Laim worked with me on the three to eleven shift, at Inglis's. He used to live facing our house in Keegan St with his mother, father, brother's Big Jimmy, Arty, Jack and sisters Eileen and Mary. Laim was married to a lovely wee girl called Maureen Toner, Dinto's daughter from Tomb St near the docks. Laim and I would often dander home together after we had finished our shift in the bakery. Dinto was a real character. Laim always said that if you offered Dinto a bowl of stew he would ask you to leave the pot and a ladle down beside him as it would save you from running in and out of the working kitchen bringing him bowls of stew and he would have finished the pot no matter what the size. Dinto could handle himself in any situation and not many would have challenged him. His nephew Hughie Toner was a merchant navy officer who was married to my half sister Kathleen Treble. They lived in Turf Lodge where unfortunately Hughie would die in tragic circumstances. He was originally from Carrick Hill and his aunt Minnie Lighting, as she was called would fit the shroud and kit out the coffins of the dead and fit out the living room with white sheets and stuff whereas now days the undertakers do all this for you. Minnie reared Hughie until he came of age. One day Hughie's sister who at the time lived a few doors up from Hughie was having a domestic with her husband and Hughie went up to calm things down. When Hughie entered the house his brother in law told him to fuck off and mind his own business. They both had words and then his brother in law threw a punch which caught Hughie on the jaw throwing Hughie backwards where he hit his head on the mantelpiece and collapsed on the floor. He didn't move a muscle and the family tried to revive him but to no avail. They sent for an ambulance but he was pronounced dead on arrival at hospital. My sister Kathleen was totally devastated understandably as she had a couple of children and just a few months previously lost a child through cot death. Now she had to face a second death in a matter of months. Hughie's brother in law was arrested and was convicted of manslaughter for which he served time. It was a terrible shame as the fellow didn't deliberately set out to kill him and the whole situation was just awful for everyone. It was just one of life's tragedies that sometimes happen. Not long after these terrible events our Kathleen and my other sister Maureen who was married to Joe Brown Senior the undertaker who sadly passed away a few years back the emigrated to Australia to start a new life. Kathleen has been back to see me a few times over the years. Our mum and stepfather passed away a few years back and our other sister Eilleen has been out in Australia from the early sixties. She lost her husband Michael to a heart attack last year. She's off on a cruise around Europe and is calling in to see the family and I before she returns to Australia.

In the year of nineteen seventy eight I was working on the grave yard shift in Inglis's and working with me were Laim McGuire, his brother Big Jack, Johnnie knock em dead Maher, Big John Mathews, Gerry Hanna, and Big Mark McGran. Mark was in his twenties and you would have strained your neck looking up at him as he stood about six feet six. The song The Monster Mash was in the hit parade at the time and the guy who sang it sounded like Boris Carloff. Mark would sing this same song over and over as he was working away putting the dough into the tin shapes before they went on the oven.

"Mark if you were singing for your dinner, you would starve to death" I would say to him and he would burst out laughing.

Tragedy lay ahead for him though, as one night when he finished his shift before me as he had started an hour before me, he headed out for a drink. Mark travelled up Eliza St and along Stewart St in order to get to the Short Strand. Just as he got to the bridge some guy jumped of a bike, pulled out a gun and shot Big Mark dead before getting back on his bike and cycling off in the direction of East Belfast. Mark was cut down in the prime of his life when he had everything to live for. He was another victim of a senseless war that should never have happened as it was forced upon us by a cruel warlord known as England who has thrived on death and destruction for centuries, especially in other peoples land.

Chapter 23

The Exploits Of Captain Crook

I can recall one time when some friends and I were sitting in The City Hibs Club when the subject of who discovered Australia came up. When the question was asked some of our company said it was Captain Cook while I said it was the Native Aborigines. However we did agree that the expansion of the British Empire as they called it, where the sun never sets comprising land masses in all the five continents was some achievement for such a small country as England. Whilst all in our company now knew of Captain Cook, I asked them did any of them know of Captain Crook, to which they all replied they hadn't, so I proceeded to educate that foolish bunch.

The year is 1850 and Captain Crook is on a plundering mission in the South Pacific Ocean. As he lands at this small island, he anchors his ship which was a man of war before he and some of his men board their small boats and begin rowing towards the island to see if there are any inhabitants around. He soon spotted a group of natives coming along the beach with this large figure in the middle of them and Captain Crook made his way towards the natives.

"Get them cannons closer because you never know what can happen" he instructed his men.

He then ordered another group of his men to search the island for any weapons of mass destruction that they might have in store.

"I nearly lost an eye on the last island we were on when the natives charged at us with these large bananas and I don't want it repeated" says Captain Crook.

He then introduced himself to the Chief through his interpreter a man named Alex Ferguson who can speak most of the lingo which sounds very much like Ulster Scotch.

"I am Captain Crook, we are from England which is far across the ocean and our great Queen Victoria sends you her regards and hopes you will become one of her subjects" said Crook and at that he slings a necklace of glass beads around the Chief's neck.

"That's a present from our Queen and she hopes you like them" explained Captain Crook.

The Chief smiled his approval and they all got stuck into a hearty meal consisting of roasted frogs legs, boiled birds eyes done in coconut milk, a fish supper out of Maggie Martins in Cromac St and last but not least a couple of pigs feet cooked of course and sent all the way over from Maggie Elder's in the Market's. After their meal the Captain produced his pipe and when the Chief enquires as to what the Captain is doing with this pipe, the Captain explains that he is smoking pot

"Let's just say it is a blow pipe" explained the Captain.

"We too have those and we use them for the purpose of knocking, monkeys out of the tree tops" replied the Chief.

"Well if you hit the monkeys with my blowpipe they will giggle themselves to death" says the Captain.

By now both men are ready to talk business and the Chief speaks first and thanks Captain Crook for travelling thousands of miles to give him a present from the Queen and to make friends. At that the Captain reveals his true intentions.

"Let's cut to the fucking chase here Chief what I am really here for is your treasures, things like any old gold mines, diamond mines or silver mines. Now you wouldn't happen to have a few of these lying around the island now would you? I'll even settle for a bag of black pearls, a hundred weight bag would do nicely.

The Chief then turns to the Captain and says.

"What if I have any of these treasures you speak of, what makes you think that I should hand them over to you?"

"Well now do you see all them cannons on the beach and my men who are armed to the teeth and what weapons do you have apart from bananas and kiwi fruit. For fuck sake wake up and smell the turtle soup Chief" the Captain says to the Chief in anger.

"I can't smell any soup" the Chief says.

"It's just an oul saying" the Captain quirks.

"I never heard any owl on the island saying that" replied the Chief

The Captain is fuming now.

"Are you for fucking real Chief, Jesus Christ you have to be the stupidest leader I have ever come across and I have sailed round the world three times and anyhow there is nothing on this island of yours and I thought Ireland was bad but at least my wife could get her free soup, veg and spuds there" said he Captain.

The Chief told The Captain through Alex Ferguson the interpreter who was looking rather pissed off as he usually does that a ship called into the island a few months ago and they said that they were from America and their Captain was called thrush or Bush. At that the Captain butted in and asked what they wanted. The Chief informed Captain Crook that the Americans had asked for the same things that he had asked for and that on leaving that they said they would call back in a few months time. Captain Crook is getting angry now.

"Don't let them back on the island" he shouts.

"The first thing they will do is install a McDonald's fast food restaurant, Kentucky fried chicken stalls, a Wall Mart super market and a Coca Cola factory and through time most of your people will end up dying of heart attacks and as time goes by some of them will go about looking like bouncy castles. The Chief then explained to the Captain that he did not have any of the mines that the Captain was seeking.

"Jesus Christ" the Captain cries.

"I will need to be going home with something because there is big money tied up in these expeditions. Are your people good workers?" the Captain asked.

The Chief replied that they were not bad workers and the Captain asked him if he could grow a couple of tobacco plantations and that his people would be paid a penny a day and all the tobacco they could chew and the Chief nodded his approval.

"Oh by the way, did these Americans give you any gifts" asked the Captain.

"Oh yes, they gave my people some chocolate and chewing gum" replied the Chief

Captain Crook explained to the Chief that the gifts were only a ploy as the Americans did that on every island they landed on. He then bids his goodbyes and indicates that he shall return soon in order to get the tobacco plantations up and running and he left behind around a dozen men to keep an eye on things and to keep him informed by carrier pigeon before sailing for home.

Captain Crook enquires from one of his officers about Alex Ferguson and how he got the job as interpreter in the first place, as the Captain says he can hardly make out a word that comes out of his mouth. The officer explained that whilst being interviewed for the position that Ferguson had told them that he speaks five languages.

"Well they all must have been scotch because he sounds very much like yer man Robbie Burns" says the Captain.

"One of the crew suggested that we should have got the Big Yin Billy Connelly and at least he might have cracked a joke now and again. However someone shouted back that he couldn't crack an egg into a fucking pan and anyhow he laughs at his own jokes" said the officer.

The Big Yin told his friends when he was starting out that he was going to be a comedian and they all laughed, they are not laughing now.

As we were sailing past Spain and the Rock of Gibraltar Ferguson shouted from the deck of the ship.

"One day I'll own part of that" and we all laughed at him.

One time he was paid a thuppenny bit short in his wages and he was going to wreak the ship and it took six sailors to hold him down. Ferguson did eventually calm down after about an hour or so but the crew had to repaint the starboard bough as his breath while screaming obscenities had stripped the paint of the side of the ship. The officer also said that Ferguson is retiring next year and that he is fed up with all the crap and that he couldn't care less who steps into his shoes, just so long as it's not that wee ginger headed git Neil Lennon.

Two weeks had passed and Captain Crook and his crew are still on the high seas when he receives a message from the island that the natives have split into two separate groups that are now at war with each other. One group wants the English to leave the island whilst the other group opposed to them includes the Chief who is over the moon with his beautiful glass beads.

"You can't leave these people alone for five minutes" the Captain says.

"We will have to turn around and head back to the island to save our men. This sort of thing shouldn't happen until we are leaving the island for good, the natives can then slaughter one another till the cows come home and who cares. Why is it that no matter what island we land on the natives always, end up fighting with one another. After all we are a friendly race of people who just want what's best for the islanders all we are seeking in return is their treasures and their lands, now that's not too much to ask for, is it? The Captain concluded.

Here follows a quote from a native inhabitant who had his land conquered by the white man.

"When the white man first came to our shores we had the land and they had the bible, after we opened our eyes we found that it was now he who possessed the land while we now had the bible and after they stole our treasures and destroyed our culture, they then made us sing that great spiritual hymn oh what a friend we have in Jesus.

Chapter 24

Five Rockets Caught Up In Rocket Attack At The Rock

We were now moving into the nineteen nineties and the troubles were continuing although they were not nearly as bad as the early seventies but they were still simmering underneath the surface none the less. One Saturday afternoon around October my brother in law Seamus Davis and I got a taxi up to the Rock Bar on the Falls Rd. We had arranged to meet up with my eldest son Michael, his brother in law Thomas Lavery and a friend of theirs. We met them in the lounge bar upstairs, apart from ourselves there were a few couples having their lunch but otherwise it was fairly quiet. There was a darts match on the television and we were enjoying the craic and the pints even better. Who should all of a sudden walk in but the RUC, Four of them all heavily armed as per usual. It appeared to me that they must have been looking for someone in particular as they looked all around then left without saying a word. Around twenty minutes later I got up to go to the toilet when I heard this unmerciful bang. It sounded like someone had slammed the main door that leads into the toilet area, then, all the lights went out. I ran back into the lounge and everyone was in a state of shock. We all bolted for the stairs and run straight down and on to the street. The crowds seemed to come out of nowhere, it was pandemonium. Rumours were doing the rounds that the Rock Bar had been bombed and that there had been fatalities and these rumours were spreading like wildfire. One of our company mentioned that we had left a table full of drinks left behind and that we go back up and finish them, I'll not tell you what I said to him. Apparently some guy got down on one knee on the Falls Rd across from the bar and fired an RPG rocket propelled grenade at the window of the top lounge in which we were sitting. The window was covered with a wire cage and luckily for us the grenade hit the apex of the wall which was made of sandstone. Had the rocket hit a couple of inches to the left the wire grill would not have stopped the propelled grenade from exploding in the lounge possibly killing or at the very least causing a lot of injuries to the patrons inside, including ourselves. Our Michael's wife Annette had phoned our house and told Patsy that we were drinking in the Rock Bar at the time of the explosion, so I phoned the house to let Patsy know that we were all safe and sound. For the life of me I cannot understand why he didn't direct his fire towards the downstairs windows, he couldn't have missed. There was a statement issued the next day from one of them loyalist groups indicating that there was a Republican meeting going on in the upstairs lounge. This was utter nonsense as I have stated before there were five of us enjoying a couple of pints and a few couples sitting having a meal and I'm a witness to that as I was in the lounge bar at the time.

Almost shot at my own door in Carrick Hill by the UVF, nearly assassinated in Donegal St by God knows who on my way to work and nearly blew to bits in the Rock Bar on the Falls Rd, I believe somebody up there likes me, I hope. Now days with the Good Friday Agreement in operation things have greatly improved for the majority of us and I know that the troubles have affected a lot of people out there some who have lost loved ones and are worse of than me. I was lucky on a few occasions and here's hoping that the troubles never return for everyone's sake. Our people need a respite and we need to try and bring the two communities together, maybe we need another James Larkin to come on the scene and achieve this just like Larkin did in the Belfast Dockers strike of 1907. Larkin united both Catholic and Protestant workers on social issues. However it didn't last long as it wasn't in some people's best interest to allow that to happen. I know it will take years but it will have to be accomplished sooner or later and if we are waiting on the Brits to bring this about we will be waiting until hell freezes over.

Now days it is all down to worldwide economics. The British Government are pumping billions into this place with no returns. I think they see it as a drain on their economy. These six counties of the province of Ulster are like a giant moneybox with a large black hole at the bottom, which sucks out all the English cash to where it disappears into another dimension never to be seen again. The riches that Britain must have amassed over the years from their rape and theft of other people's lands must run into the trillions only for it all to disappear down a large black hole called Northern Ireland. World capitalism and the banking system are in meltdown and we are still stuck in this recession, the worst one I have seen in my lifetime and there seems to be no light at the end of the tunnel. Catholics have mostly worked in the building trade due to the fact that the ship building and aircraft factories were out of bounds to them. It was the Catholics here in the North who depended on the building sites for a steady income but it took a big hit when the property market collapsed and it will take a right few years for it to return to some kind of normality. I wouldn't hold out much hope of it happening anytime soon. Now days there are tradesmen driving taxis for a living but mortgages have to be paid and food needs to be put on the table. They say now days if you need a plumber or a plasterer you can just call a taxi, that is just a joke but there is no joy in driving a taxi for a living as my eldest son Michael would tell you.

After the seven marriages of my own children, five weddings of my grandchildren, first communions, confirmations, christenings and birthdays, Patsy and I are broke but who cares because we thoroughly enjoyed every minute of it. We now have eighteen grandchildren and nine great grandchildren, so you see what we started. You think that when all your children get married and leave home that your life will be a lot easier, are you having a laugh, they just bring more children back with them. On Christmas Day we have to employ a car park attendant to direct the cars in and out of the street. Margaret, Henrietta and Daniel all live up in Glengormley within close proximity to each other, Michael lives just off the Glen Road, Leo is in Moyard, Sharon is in Andersonstown, Denise lives off the Lisburn Road and Geraldine lives facing us in Carrick Hill.

Chapter 25

The Old Market Is Replaced By The New

The old Market's is long gone now replaced with new housing but the unemployment in the area is still a factor as there is no Inglis's bakery and the cattle yards and the shirt factories have long gone. Some of the old street names have been changed to make way for the new but I suppose nothing stays the same forever as the old saying goes and maybe more's the pity. It was a privilege and an honour to be brought up and reared in the Market, with so many fond memories of the place and the people I grew up with and have met down through the years. In the old

Market people would look out for each other and try and help each other out when anyone was in trouble and I often wonder will those days ever return. I for one certainly hope so but alas times change as do people and the chances of the old community spirit that we enjoyed ever returning looks ever more bleak. People have more money in their pockets these days and in a lot of cases have more than one car at their door but that's all they have as they live behind closed doors and take their security measures to protect their homes from crime. We didn't need any of these so called security measures back in the day as all our doors were open to all in the neighbourhood and crime for the most part was non existent. We may have had nothing but we didn't steal our neighbour's goods but in saying that there was nothing to steal we were all skint. Life may have been hard but we certainly made the most of what we had and enjoyed it to the full.

I can recall an instance when I was talking to a fellow I know, it was around the mid nineties and he told me that his partner was pregnant and that he was going to have to get a house and that he was off to Andytown to meet with the estate agent to enquire about a house in one of the Rock Streets that was on the market for fifteen thousand pounds which seemed virtually half price at the time. I bumped into him a few days later and asked how the house hunting went.

"Well Dan I asked the agent what the average monthly payment would be on a fifteen thousand mortgage and he informed me that the house in question did not have any mortgage facilities and that it could only be purchased by cash buyers" he said

"And why was that" I asked.

"Apparently any house without an extension that still has the outside toilet is deemed unfit for human habitation and officially by law you can not obtain a mortgage to purchase such a property. Can you believe that Dan? We were all brought up in illegal houses back in the day and with larger families than the average family now days."

"Who makes these fucking laws" I replied.

"Well Dan I cant answer that one but I do know that there are tribes that live in the Siberian forests who follow the rain dear all year round and put every part of the animals they kill to good use and they move their deer skin tents with them that they use as homes. Now they may clean their arse with a leaf in the forest, instead of Andrex but what the fuck apparently it's legal and free of stupid bureaucrats that make up stupid laws such as telling me that a house with a flushing toilet is officially unfit for human habitation" he said.

Chapter 26

Two Very Different Women

A lot of the people from the Market have moved further on up the Ormeau Road to live, as after all the Market population was expanding. The news had just come in that Maggie Thatcher the former Prime Minister of Britain had passed away at the age of eighty seven. To some she was called the Iron Lady and to others she was called the Wicked Witch of Westminster or the Evil Empress among other things. You can take your pick but one thing for sure is that she was the most hated woman in England at one time and probably still is to most. She was certainly a thorn in the side of the Irish people of the north of Ireland and the majority of the English working classes. Her leadership resulted in the deaths of ten republican hunger strikers in the H Blocks of Long Kesh. She was also the cause of mass unemployment in many of the industries of her own country, from the miners to the steel workers, the railroads and also the motorcar manufacturing industry. She privatized everything in her path and the working classes were just like pawns on a chess board to be wiped off with the back of her hand. With many housing estates left decimated and factories crumbling into dust, I just wonder what her logic was in creating all this mayhem. She destroyed the trade unions and they still haven't recovered to this day. I can remember watching the news shortly after the Brighton Bombing had occurred and when the reporter asked member of the public in England for his views on the incident he most certainly got his answer.

"As an Englishman I've got no time for the likes of the IRA but it's just a pity they missed that bitch on this occasion" was his reply.

I guess that's what happens when you put a woman in the driving seat, there is bound to be a collision one way or the other. This doesn't apply to all you safe lady drivers out there, if there are any. I have to keep myself right here as most of my daughters drive, well they certainly drive me round the bend at any rate.

Of all the people I have admired down through the years Bernadette Devlin who was once a member of parliament at Westminster really sticks out. In my reckoning she should have been made the President of Ireland, its still not too late. This woman has been through the mill. I admired the stand she took when she stood shoulder to shoulder with the people in Derry's Bogside fighting against the Orange forces of the State namely the RUC and the B Specials. Then off course there was that famous slap on the face she gave to Mr Reginald Mauldling who was the Home Affairs Minister and in charge of Britain's Northern Ireland policy at the time. It was shortly after the British Paratroopers had murdered thirteen people at a Derry Civil Rights march and while Mauldling was given the floor to defend their murderous actions Bernadette was denied the right to speak on the issue by the Speaker of the House. So much for the right to free speech under British Democracy eh! Then came the attempted murder bid on both herself and her husband by a loyalist hit squad. Another army unit that was in the area at the time rendered first aid to the victims before getting them airlifted to hospital to try and save their lives, luckily they pulled through. Now that's a hard one to get your head around. Firstly send out a squad to kill them and then send another to save their lives. Maybe the loyalists on duty that day forgot to inform their RUC Special Branch handlers that they were going to be busy. Bernadette was a socialist through and through and was always speaking up for the working class people and their interests, fighting unjust laws for everyone, no matter what their class or creed. Though I guess she would be seen as too much of a left winger to become President of Ireland. Is it such a crime to hold socialist aspirations and left wing views? It would appear to be so even in this modern era where they keep telling us that we have freedom and free speech. Ok maybe the powers that be won't execute us for treason as was the case back in the day when they executed Thomas Payne but they certainly despise our ideals.

Chapter 27

Family reunions

On the seventeenth of April my sister Eileen called in to stay with the family and I before she was due to fly to Dubai, where she would spend four days before returning back home to Australia. She spent a fortnight with us and I must say it was great to see her. It had been six years since I last seen her, it was two thousand and six to be exact and on that occasion she was accompanied by her husband Michael. However on this occasion she was home to spread Michael's ashes in London where he was born. Although he was reared in Scotland and you wouldn't half know when you listened to his broad Scottish accent. During her visit we didn't get to visit as many places as I would have wished, as the weather was up the left, cold wet and windy as usual. She had been on a cruise since February that year and would not return home to Australia till May. In the fifties she stayed down at the Market with Aunt Kitty and I. My mother and sisters Kathleen and Maureen and my younger brother Joe would also stay with us on occasions. Maureen would go on to marry Joe Brown the undertaker. A few years after marrying, they separated and Maureen went off to Australia with a fella called Ned Mulgrew from Ardoyne. Coincidently a few years down the road our youngest daughter Sharon would marry Joe's nephew who was also called Joe and they now live in Riverdale just off the Andersonstown Road with their three children.

Charlie the stepfather was banged up in jail in Liverpool, where he was serving time for robbing a jewellers shop. Apparently he chucked a brick through the plate glass window and when asked by the judge why he did it his reply was that he needed the money. Charlie was a real character all right. Our mother didn't fancy staying in Liverpool so she asked Aunt Kitty if she could come and stay with her until she got herself sorted out and put her name on the housing list. Eileen told me that she thoroughly enjoyed her time in the Market when she had her wee job in one of the shirt factories on the Dublin Road. Our Kath also got herself a job in Grevis's Mill on the Falls Road while Mum and our Maureen got jobs working in the canteen of the Belfast City Hospital. My mother eventually got herself a house in New Barnsley on the Springfield Road facing Ballymurphy. However when the troubles broke out my mother Charlie and my younger brother all decided to emigrate to Australia and two years later my two sisters Kath and Maureen would join them. Mum would come back over in the late seventies for a holiday and she would stay with her sister Hanna and my two eldest sisters Marie and Bernadette would join her. Our Marie lived in Wales and Bernie was residing in America at the time, so it was like a wee family reunion with them all back in Belfast at the same time. Carrick Hill is where I live now and have done for the past forty years. It is a small estate at the bottom of the Shankill Road and next door to the New Lodge Area. You step out your front door and you're in the city centre more or less. There are around three hundred families living in the Hill as we call it. My grandfather and grandmother and their families lived in the old Carrick Hill in the early nineteen hundreds. However soon after my grandfather was killed in the First World War my grandmother moved to number one Milford St in the Falls Road Area and that would be where my grandmother ended her days in the late sixties.

Chapter 28

A Great Community Spirit

Around the same time Patsy and I moved to our new home in Stanhope Drive and the estate was then called Unity Flats and it was a two story complex. We lived on the upper story in a three bedroom maisonette which was lovely and warm in the summer but absolutely freezing in the winter and it took a fortune to heat it due to the flat roof. Patsy's family also lived close by, her sister Madeline and brother's Seamus and Leo Davis just lived a couple of streets away and her other sister Colette just lived nearby in Stephen Street. The children hadn't got that far to travel to school which was situated in North Queen St. They were later to build a nursery school in Stanhope Drive for the three year olds and then later again they also converted an old church in Regent St into a community centre where Patsy would eventually acquire a job. It was ideal for both of us as I worked in the afternoons and Patsy worked in the mornings which meant she would be there for the children when they got out of school around three thirty. Some of the local shops were Al Austin's confectioners shop, Lizzie Drummonds fruit shop on Upper Library St , Jimmy Creas confectioners shop, Paddy Jordan's who sold fish and chips on Clifton St, Tommy Campbell's Butchers and the home bakery Paddy Floods. Then you also had the Tavern bar at the lower end of Peter's Hill. The owners and staff of these businesses worked all hours to facilitate our community right through the height of the troubles when they were prime targets for robbers and loyalist killer gangs. These men and women were putting their lives at risk to serve our community and should be honoured as such.

There were some great community leaders in the Hill at that time and Jean O'Rielly comes to mind here as she worked in the community centre with the children of the area but sadly Jean passed away at an early age and she was sadly missed. Patsy also worked in the community centre but retired before the new centre was built. Frank Dipper Dempsey was to take over the running of the new community centre. In the early years there were bus runs for the children and summer schemes that lasted for six weeks the whole time they were off school which was great but alas all of these schemes were to be cut as there was no budget for them due to the economic downturn. Emanuel Conway was another community worker who had a lot of time for the children of the area. He would run parties and games to entertain the kids during the summer months. All through the marching season which would last from around Easter until about September the residents of the small Carrick Hill community had to endure being hemmed in every time the Orange Order decided it was time for a march. Access to and from the estate was severely restricted on these occasions. You would need to see it to believe it especially in this day and age. From early morning police Land Rovers and military armoured vehicles would block all the entrances and exits to and from the area and there were always at least one helicopter hovering overhead. It was reminiscent of a scene from the

Gazza Strip or Vietnam, take your pick. The people of Carrick Hill have had to endure these sectarian marches for decades now and they really don't deserve it.

The cops have now stopped the orange supporters from walking down Clifton St on the footpath beside the bands which caused a lot of trouble in the past and although this change is to be welcomed there remains a lot of work to be done. These same Orangemen have on numerous occasions been seen singing sectarian songs in and around St Patrick's church in a clear breech of the Parades Commission rulings. Now these Orangemen get of their buses at Carlisle Circus they then walk the two hundred yards or so past Carrick Hill and St Patrick's before boarding the bus which has now moved to the bottom of Donegal St to pick them up and bring them on to their destination. Then they repeat the process only in reverse when they disembark from the buses at the bottom of Donegal St before marching up Clifton St to get back on board their buses at Carlisle Circus for the journey home, now work that one out. I would love to know who is paying for all this policing and surely the Orange Order must take responsibility for all this disruption and be made to cough up towards the costs of policing and then I guess we would have fewer sectarian parades. They must sit down and hold face to face talks with the resident's group's full stop. They have never endorsed the Good Friday Agreement but then they would say neither has the various republican groups but I believe the State brands them groups as terrorists, what's the difference. The reason they will not sit down and talk is simple, they believe that their opinion is the only opinion that counts and that this is their wee country and no one else's and that they can walk where they want and do not need to recognize the Parades Commission or any residents groups. I would say to the Orange Order.

"Do you really assume that the British Government will continue to pay for the astronomical policing bills related to parading through the flashpoint areas while we are all currently feeling the effects in this economic downturn when everything else is going to the wall. Everyone is suffering here due to the cuts so what makes you think you are any different."

The way I see it, the Orange Order are stuck in the eighteenth century and they seem to find it very difficult to break away from their old outdated beliefs and traditions. Now this is very sad indeed because I believe they could make a great contribution to a lasting peace and reconciliation and a shared future in our society if they would just make the effort. Maybe they should think of the children, their own children included because I believe it is the duty of all of us to make this achievable.

We had some great neighbours that lived beside us in the old Unity Flats such as Brian and Kathleen O'Rourke who lived facing us, Mrs Teresa Brown, Mrs Belle Moore, Mr and Mrs McKeown, David and Mary Johnston, Paddy and Cassie McMahon, the Dorian's and Mrs Loughlin to name but a few. A new housing project has replaced the old maisonettes in and around the Carrick Hill area and I now reside in one of the new builds, a four bedroom house with a garden. There are built in eco systems in the new houses which is a far cry from the old ice boxes we used to live in.

Chapter 29

To Hell And Back

"To hell and back" sounds like a quote from one of the old Audy Murphy war films. Back in June this year my younger daughter asked me if I could collect the two grandchildren out of school as she had to go into town. As we were approaching my car I had to stop and get my breath back, Jesus Christ I thought to myself what's happening to me. I have never experienced anything like that before. I was standing at the school wall with my two grandchildren and Bernie Carlisle, a lovely wee girl who lives not very far from my youngest daughter Sharon in Riverdale was making her way round home with her granddaughter. She Stopped, and asked.

"What's wrong with you Danny you look a terrible colour are you feeling Ok."

"I am a bit short of breath" I said hoarsely.

"I'll better get these kids down to their granny" I said and thanked Bernie for her concern before promptly leaving as I was not feeling great at all. I made an appointment to see the doctor that Friday at six o'clock and after examining me he told me to return and see him on Tuesday of the following week and gave me a prescription for a fluid tablet. Come Saturday morning our Hetty called in to get her tea before she went out to work as she is a carer for the elderly and I told her that I had a prescription that I needed to collect from the chemist.

"Give it to me because I've a couple of prescriptions to collect so I'll get it for you when I'm out" and with that she jumped in the car and headed over to the Shore Road to get the prescriptions. Hetty told her mate who was working in the chemist shop about me going to the doctor and about how I would be gasping for breath after only walking a short distance.

"What age is your father" the girl in the chemist says.

"He is seventy four years old" replied our Hetty and her friend told her that she should bring me to the accident and emergency at the Mater Hospital as soon as possible.

Hetty rang my eldest daughter Geraldine and told her to get herself ready and accompany us to the Mater. I was getting myself ready to go out for a drink as I do every Saturday afternoon when Hetty informed me the she wanted to bring me up to the A&E at the Mater and I must admit I was not very keen on the idea.

"I'll go up on Monday" was my reply and at that the wife came out from the working kitchen with a rolling pin in her hand. Now I know your probably thinking that she was doing a little bit of baking.

"I must get you a new rolling pin dear, that one looks to have a lot of rough edges around it and I'll also pick up that new steam iron I promised you"

"But I already have one" replied Patsy.

"Sure I'll get you another ironing board as well and you can walk up the middle of the two ironing boards with a steam iron in each hand and then you can iron two shirts at the same time" I said and with that she took a run at me with the rolling pin raised above her head

"Hetty your Mummy's going to whack me with that rolling pin" said I laughing.

I was trying to get out of going to the hospital but to no avail.

"Listen Da just lets go up and get you checked out and it shouldn't take us more than half an hour" said Hetty.

"Right but if its any more than that I'm gone" I replied.

We drove through the Mater Hospital gates at around two thirty and I went straight to the A&E department and checked in and for some strange reason the department was unusually empty apart from the staff who were on duty. I had no sooner sat down when my name was called. I went straight into the nearest cubicle where I was instructed to remove my top and they promptly began conducting the various tests. After they had concluded the tests they informed my two daughters Hetty, Geraldine and I that my heart was racing too fast. I only wish I could have said the same about most of the horses that I have gambled on down through the years. One of the doctors suggested that they inquire about the availability of an empty bed as I would need to be kept in due to the fact that they needed to conduct more tests. I was not taking too kindly to the idea of staying in the hospital overnight but little did I realize what lay ahead of me. After many scans and tests Dr Clements who was the consultant who had studied the results called me into his office to explain his findings. He informed me that I had an aortic aneurysm that had a seven and a half centimetre fracture. This aortic artery goes from the heart down to the legs and up to the brain and I asked Dr Clements if it was dangerous.

"You have a ticking time bomb in your chest Mr Mulcahy which could go at any time, there is a weakness in the aortic wall and it allows a section to expand like a balloon, aortic aneurysms are slow to grow but they can be fatal if they rupture. You also have a leaking valve going into the heart"

"Have you any good news for me Doc" said I laughing and not realizing how dangerous the situation really was. There actually was one piece of good news believe it or not, he informed me that I had a healthy heart and that my arteries were clear of any disease so at least that was something.

"You also have a big operation ahead of you Mr Mulcahy so in the meantime we will concentrate on that.

"Is there any risks involved Doctor" I asked.

"There are risks in everything even crossing the road but you will be in good hands and that I can assure you" he said and with that we shook hands and I left his office and went back to my ward.

A fortnight later I was on my way over to the Royal Victoria Hospital. I was placed in a small side ward in order to prevent me from contracting any infections prior to my surgery. Patsy's younger sister Colette who works in the Royal Maternity Canteen brought me a breakfast over to the ward and it was on a plate the size of a bin lid. Now anyone who knows Colette can tell you she will stand over you till you finish the lot but the next day I had to tell her that I had to go on a fast as I could be brought into surgery for my operation at any time.

The big day had finally arrived and they transferred me over to the house of horrors as I called at the old part of the Royal beside the statue of Queen Vic. On the morning of the operation they got me prepared and I received an injection to calm me down and half an hour later I felt like singing after feeling the effects of the drug that they had administered into my system. I was wheeled into the theatre at around eight am and after approximately ten hours on the chopping board I was eventually removed to the recovery room. About an hour later when they were examining me they discovered that there was a blood leak from the newly replaced heart valve and panic stations set in so I was rushed back into the theatre where they proceeded to open me up for the second time. As you can imagine I was totally unaware of what was going on due to the effect of the anaesthetic I was under. Our Michael, Daniel and Leo later informed me that they had agreed not to mention anything about the complication to their mother as they were of the opinion that it would only cause her undue stress. A few worrying hours later and much to the relief of my family they had found the cause. Apparently there are two different methods used for conducting heart surgery, one is for a zipper down the chest to get at the heart and the other which is the one I went through is when they go in at the side underneath the armpit. This method leaves the chest with very little scaring and someone mentioned to me that they also freeze the brain and with a head the size of mine it would take some fucking ice cube to freeze this one, more like a fucking ice berg I laughed. They also bring your temperature right down to minimize the risk of a stroke and to prevent the body from going into cardiac arrest or shock. I think at this point that I was experiencing nightmare dreams when I was under the surgeon's knife. I experienced this weird dream where my five daughters all piled into this large hearse which would put you in mind of the film Darby O'Gill and the Little People, it was lashing out of the heavens and it was dark and windy and my daughters all had these black umbrellas that matched their black dresses. In the background I could hear a song, it was a nineteen fifties hit for Little Jimmy Brown. Bong Bong and the chapel bells were ringing as the words went sung by a choir. I've heard worse, well not much worse.

After I came out of theatre I lay in the recovery room for a few days before being transferred to the rehabilitation ward. I called it the cold turkey ward for it certainly felt that way when you were coming of the drugs. You were being fed all kinds of drugs from heroin to you name it. I was imagining all kinds of shit, that my sister in law's two daughters were nurses working on the ward and that my grandson Connor was the male nurse who was giving the orders to the other nurses. Also friends of mine were walking by my bed dressed as cleaners and each morning when I awoke I imagined that my bed was in a different ward. I firmly believe that before a person undergoes such operations that they should be made aware of the effects that these drugs will have on your system rather than finding out the hard way. I was also insisting that my family take me home but they kept informing me that I wasn't fit enough for my wife Patsy to look after me. I kept telling the doctors and nurses that I wanted to sign myself out but everyone was ignoring me and looking back on it how could you blame them. Our Denise maintains that on one occasion when she came up to visit me in the hospital that I was threatening to hit her for not organizing someone with a car to take me home. Now I would never harm a hair on any of my children's heads but what kind of demons must be lurking in the dark recesses of our minds only to surface when they are unleashed by some of the most powerful drugs known to man, God only knows. I spent another few days in the house of horrors struggling with my inner demons and praying for a speedy recovery so that I could go home as soon as possible. The following week I was moved back to my old ward where it had all started and it wouldn't be long until I was out. Towards the end of the week the house doctor was doing his rounds and he called into the ward and informed me that I could go home and happy days I thought to myself.

The weather was warm as it was a beautiful sunny day and our Michael had just called in to visit me.

"Right I'm going home" I said.

It was the eighth of July and by God it was great to be home. Patsy had a meal ready for me but I couldn't eat it as I had no appetite due to the fact that my taste buds were not functioning normally and I had lost nearly two and a half stone. My son Daniel would lift me in and out of the bath and up and down the stairs. Patsy had to wash my hair as there was no feeling in my right arm and I was told that it would take around six months or more after the operation before I would get back to some kind of normality and believe me they weren't too far off the mark. I knew that I wouldn't be driving for a lot of months and now my license needs to be renewed every three years now that I have turned seventy five and you also need to get your photos renewed and just last week I posed for the photos. I got our Sharon to collect them out of the chemist and when she handed me the envelope with the photos I took one look at them and gave them straight back to her.

"He has given you the wrong photos, they are somebody's great granddads photos" I said to her.

"No Daddy, your name is on the back of the envelope and don't forget you are a great granddad" she said.

"Then the chemist should have gone to Specsavers" I laughed as I was just winding her up, sure if you don't laugh you will cry.

This autobiography is dedicated to my family and my son in laws and daughter in laws. Thomas Loughlin who is married to our eldest daughter Geraldine, Annette who is married to my eldest son Michael, Ciaran Gallagher who is married to our Margaret. Tony Lynch married to Henrietta, our Leo who is married to Michelle. Paul Skeffington who is married to our Denise and our wee Sharon is married to Young Joe Brown and last but not least our youngest son Daniel who is dating his girlfriend Ciara McCusker.

Also to my large family circle and all my friends whom I have met down through the years

(All three of them that is, just in case this memoir takes off and I make a fortune when Stephen Spielberg comes a calling around Carrick Hill way)

THE END

St Colmans Primary
That's me front & center

My Mother and Father
Mary & Henry

Aunt Kitty
Friend Robert

Hanna, My Mother & Aunt Alice

Kathleen, Bernie, Marie Eileen, Danny

Me and John Treble

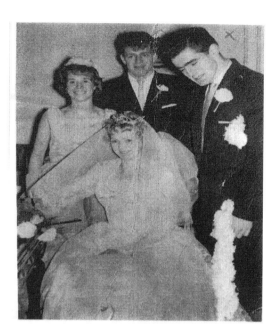

My Wedding Day
Patrica Mulcahy, Danny Mulcahy
Martha Leckey, Micheal Davis

Eddy Meighan, Patsy Mccormack,
Dushas Parker, Patrica Davis, Danny
Mulcahy

My Daughters and Sons

(Margaret)Geraldine
And Margaret

Denise, Sharon
And Hetty

Daniel
And
Michael

Leo

Printed in Great Britain
by Amazon